BASIC / NOT BORING
SOCIAL STUDIES SKILLS

U.S.
HISTORY

Grades 6–8+

Inventive Exercises to Sharpen
Skills and Raise Achievement

Series Concept & Development
by Imogene Forte & Marjorie Frank
Exercises by Leland Graham & Frankie Long

Incentive Publications, Inc.
Nashville, Tennessee

About the cover:
Bound resist, or tie dye, is the most ancient known method of fabric surface design. The brilliance of the basic tie dye design on this cover reflects the possibilities that emerge from the mastery of basic skills.

Illustrated by Kathleen Bullock
Cover art by Mary Patricia Deprez, dba Tye Dye Mary®
Cover design by Marta Drayton, Joe Shibley, and W. Paul Nance
Edited by Anna Quinn

ISBN 978-0-86530-373-7

4   5   6   7   8   9   10   07

PRINTED IN THE UNITED STATES OF AMERICA
www.incentivepublications.com

TABLE OF CONTENTS

CELEBRATE BASIC SOCIAL STUDIES SKILLS

Basic does not mean boring! There certainly is nothing dull about . . .

  . . . looking in on some of the great triumphs, tragedies, surprises, and changes in the United States' past

  . . . learning about slaves, robber barons, witches, astronauts, and cowboys

  . . . clearing up confusion about which events in the past happened when

  . . . finding out who the VIPs are in American history, and what's so great about them

  . . . getting an inside look at two wild decades known as the "roaring twenties" and "the sixties"

  . . . discovering who really discovered America

  . . . figuring out who the United States fought in which war (and why)

  . . . tracking down famous historical quotes so you'll know, "Who said that?"

  . . . telling the difference between cold wars and hot wars

  . . . becoming something of an expert on the famous landmarks and monuments of the U.S.

The idea of celebrating the basics is just what it sounds like—enjoying and improving social studies skills. The pages that follow are full of exercises for students that will help to review and strengthen specific, basic skills in the content area of United States history. This is not just another ordinary "fill-in-the-blanks" way to learn. The high-interest exercises put students to work applying a rich assortment of many key facts and concepts about many aspects of U.S. history. Students will do this work while enjoying fun and challenging activities about discoveries and disputes, famous persons and places, and world-changing accomplishments, successes, and tragedies.

The pages in this book can be used in many ways:
- for individual students to sharpen a particular skill
- with a small group needing to relearn or strengthen a skill
- as an instructional tool for teaching a skill to any size group
- by students working on their own
- by students working under the direction of an adult

Each page may be used to introduce a new skill, to reinforce a skill, or even to assess a student's performance of a skill. And, there's more than just the great student activities! You will also find an appendix of resources helpful for students and teachers—including a ready-to-use test on U.S. history skills and content.

As students take on the challenges of these adventures with history, they will sharpen their mastery of basic skills and enjoy learning to the fullest. As you watch them check off the basic U.S. history skills and knowledge they've strengthened, you can celebrate with them!

SKILLS CHECKLIST FOR U.S. HISTORY

✔	SKILL	PAGE(S)
	Identify groups of indigenous people in the Americas	11
	Identify key events and issues in U.S. history involving Native Americans	11, 17, 22, 29
	Identify key events and persons involved in the European discoveries of the Americas	10, 12
	Describe reasons why various groups came to the Americas	10, 11, 15
	Identify characteristics of different American colonies and describe colonial life	13–16
	Identify features of significant documents of the new government	19
	Identify and describe causes, key persons, and events in the Revolutionary War	18, 19
	Describe key persons and events in the Westward Movement	20, 22, 26, 29
	Identify key aspects of the periods of slavery & abolition	23
	Identify key aspects of the Manifest Destiny concept	26
	Describe key events and issues surrounding the Civil War & Reconstruction	24, 25
	Describe key events and changes due to the rise of industrialism in the United States	27, 28
	Describe causes, alliances, events, and effects of World War I	30–32
	Describe key events and features of the 1920s	32
	Describe key causes, events, and effects of the Great Depression	33
	Describe key aspects and significance of the New Deal	34
	Identify causes leading up to World War II	35
	Describe key events, places, and persons of World War II	35
	Describe key features of the post World War II years	36
	Define the Cold War and describe its causes, key events, and effects	36, 37
	Identify location and issues of the Korean War	38
	Identify events of the 1960s	39
	Identify and describe features and events of the Civil Rights Movement	44
	Identify persons and events related to space exploration	41
	Identify causes, events, and issues of the war in Vietnam	40
	Identify key figures in U.S. history	10, 12, 13, 27-29, 32, 37, 39, 40-43, 45, 46
	Make and read timelines of major events in U.S. history	35, 40
	Identify famous quotes from U.S. history	45
	Identify and locate significant U.S. landmarks and monuments	46, 47
	Identify significant American inventions and inventors	48

U.S. HISTORY

Skills Exercises

WHO REALLY DISCOVERED AMERICA?

For years the most common response to this question has been "Christopher Columbus, of course!" But actually, there were at least three discoveries of America. (Some archaeological clues suggest that there may have been even more visitors to America.) How much do you know about these discoveries? Fill in the missing words to complete the summary descriptions below. Use words from the box of current archeological theories at the bottom of the page. (A word may be used more than once.)

FIRST DISCOVERY

About ——— 1 ——— years ago, people from the northern part of the continent of ——— 2 ——— came to the area of North America that is now the state of ——— 3 ——— . Today, a narrow strip of water about 50 miles wide, called the ——— 4 ——— , separates Asia from North America. But during the ——— 5 ——— , much of the northern part of North America was covered by ——— 6 ——— . With so much water frozen into ice, the ocean level was low and land was exposed, forming a natural ——— 7 ——— between Asia and North America. Asian ——— 8 ——— and ——— 9 ——— crossed this bridge and spread out, forming many societies and establishing cultures throughout the continent.

SECOND DISCOVERY

About ——— 10 ——— years ago, ——— 11 ——— sailors, who had originally come across the ——— 12 ——— Ocean from ——— 13 ——— to Greenland, found their way down to the northeastern coast of what is now the country of ——— 14 ——— and an island off the coast, presently called ——— 15 ——— . The discoverer of this part of North America was thought to be ——— 16 ——— , the son of the famous Eric The Red.

THIRD DISCOVERY

About ——— 17 ——— years ago, a sailor by the name of ——— 18 ——— , from the country of ——— 19 ——— thought he could get to ——— 20 ——— and The ——— 21 ——— by sailing west. He crossed the ——— 22 ——— Ocean with three ships, paid for by Queen ——— 23 ——— and King ——— 24 ——— of ——— 25 ——— . In the year ——— 26 ——— , the first land he saw was the island of ——— 27 ——— in the South Atlantic Ocean. Later he sailed further south to a larger island, known today as ——— 28 ——— , and then eastward to another large island which he named ——— 29 ——— , which means the Spanish Isle. Today this island holds the countries of ——— 30 ——— and the ——— 31 ——— .

1000	San Salvador	Norway	Newfoundland
500	Bering Strait	Atlantic	land bridge
30,000	Viking	Dominican Republic	Haiti
1498	Ferdinand	Pacific	China
1492	Hispaniola	Christopher Columbus	people
Cuba	Spain	Ice Ages	animals
Indies	Asia	Canada	
Isabella	Leif Ericson	Italy	
Canada	Alaska	glaciers	

Name

WHO WAS HERE FIRST?

Sometimes we think of American history as beginning with the explorations or "discoveries" made by the Europeans. But well-developed cultures with thousands of people inhabited the North American continent long before the Europeans arrived. These people are referred to as indigenous people, meaning people "native to an area." The indigenous inhabitants that were here before the Europeans were the Native American Indians. The map below shows the location of these societies throughout North America. In general, these cultures can be divided into groups according to geographical location. For each location described, write the names of several tribes and find some information about how the people lived and found food. Use a separate piece of paper for your descriptions.

NATIVE AMERICAN GROUPS

Far North/Subarctic/Arctic
(Northern Canada and Alaska)

Northwest
(coastal areas from Northern California and north)

Southwest
(Arizona, New Mexico, northern Texas)

California
(western and southern California)

Mexico and Central America

Great Basin
(plateaus and lands between Rocky Mountains and Pacific Ocean)

Great Plains
(grasslands between Rocky Mountains and Mississippi River)

Eastern Woodlands
(land east of the Mississippi)

Name

CRUCIAL CROSSINGS

Most American students learn that "in 1492 Columbus sailed the Ocean Blue." Who else made other significant journeys to the "New World"? Were they all looking for gold? In search of a "short cut" to the riches of the East? The puzzle below reintroduces some of the explorers and the areas of the New World they explored. Use the clues to complete the puzzle.

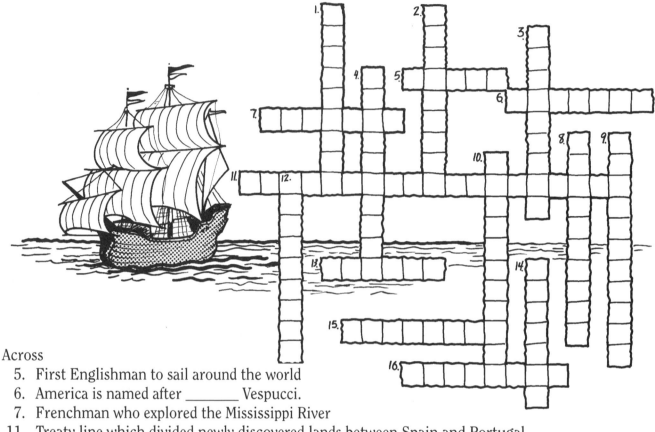

Across

5. First Englishman to sail around the world
6. America is named after _____ Vespucci.
7. Frenchman who explored the Mississippi River
11. Treaty line which divided newly discovered lands between Spain and Portugal
13. Jolliet and Marquette explored the Mississippi River for this country.
15. Italian who sailed under the flag of Spain
16. _____ and de Soto both crossed into the area now known as Texas at the same time.

Down

1. An Italian named Giovanni Caboto who was sponsored by England and sailed under the name of _____
2. An early Italian explorer after whom a New York bridge was named
3. Samuel de _____ explored the St. Lawrence River
4. A Spaniard, Juan Cabrilho, sailed along this state's coast.
8. Gulf explored and named by Jacques Cartier
9. River discovered by the Spanish explorer Hernando de Soto
10. Explorer sponsored by Holland and England
12. This English queen challenged Spain for control of the New World
14. Section of North America named by Ponce de Leon

Name

FROM DISASTER TO DEMOCRACY

POSSIBLE SCORE:
100

One of the earliest attempts to establish a settlement in America was undertaken by Sir Walter Raleigh. He sent a group to start a colony on an island called Roanoke, off the coast of what is now North Carolina. The purpose of the colony was to find gold. There was no gold, other disasters followed, and the colony was a failure. But the charter for the colony set a precedent for future settlements in the New World. The underlying concept of this and other early settlements was "government by consent of the people being governed." The following statements all relate to what is known as the Colonial Period of U.S. history. Each statement below has been assigned a point value. Work with a partner or alone for twenty minutes. See how many points you can gather by writing a QUESTION which fits each answer.

5 Points
1. The Puritans and Pilgrims came to the New World in search of this.

5 Points
2. The New World's first permanent colony.

5 Points
3. These are four of the settlements started where a river joined the ocean.

10 Points
4. ". . . that he who will not work shall not eat," said _____ to the settlers of _____ .

10 Points
5. She was the first European born in America.

10 Points
6. Two groups of people brought to the New World to work for free.

20 Points
12. These men were responsible for founding the colonies of Pennsylvania, Georgia, New Jersey, Connecticut, and Rhode Island.

_____
_____
_____
_____

10 Points
11. This country established Fort Christina along the Delaware River.

10 Points
10. The major Dutch settlement in the New World.

YOUR SCORE:

5 Points
7. This mountain range lies directly west of the thirteen original colonies.

5 Points
8. This document written in 1620 set forth the rules and regulations of the Plymouth settlement.

5 Points
9. In 1632, George Calvert founded this colony as a haven for Roman Catholics.

Name _____

THE 13 ORIGINALS

The original thirteen colonies are pictured on the map using the current boundaries of the states that grew from them. Use the map and other references to complete the following:

I. Label each of the thirteen English colonies on the map.

II. Shade the three groups of colonies: New England (green); Middle (orange); Southern (yellow).

III. Locate and label: Atlantic Ocean; Long Island Sound; Delaware Bay; Chesapeake Bay; Cape Hatteras; and Cape Cod.

IV. Locate and label the following sites: Salem; Providence; Jamestown; Williamsburg; Boston; Plymouth; Savannah; Hartford; New Haven; Portsmouth; Philadelphia; and Charleston.

V. Tell which of the original thirteen colonies fits each description:

_____ 1. The first colony founded

_____ 2. Home to Jamestown, first settlement

_____ 3. Originally known as New Sweden

_____ 4. Formed by Puritan preacher, Roger Williams

_____ 5. Home of Harvard, the first university in the new world

_____ 6. Two colonies where tobacco was an important crop

_____ 7. Originally called New Netherland

_____ 8. Formed for people who couldn't pay their debts

_____ 9. Had first elected lawmaking body, House of Burgesses

_____ 10. Founded for Quakers by William Penn

_____ 11. Two colonies formed in 1663

_____ 12. The last of the original 13, founded in 1732

_____ 13. Banished Anne Hutchinson for challenging the authority of Puritan leaders

Name

14

PREACHERS, PROFITEERS, & PRISONERS

People made the long journey to the New World for different reasons. Some were in debt or in trouble and wanted a new life. Some were escaping religious persecution. Others wanted gold or hoped for other riches. The original thirteen colonies are often grouped according to geographic location as the New England Colonies, the Middle Colonies, and the Southern Colonies. Another way of grouping these colonies is to look at the reasons for their founding.

I. Place each of the thirteen colonies in one or more of the categories below according to reasons for its founding. Use your history textbook, encyclopedia, or any other resources you need.

RELIGIOUS FREEDOM

PROFIT AND TRADE

POLITICAL FREEDOM

HOME FOR DEBTORS

II. Make two generalizations from these groupings.

_____

_____

_____

_____

Name

WHICH WITCH HUNT?

Witches are a topic that interest many people. They were especially of interest during the Salem Witch Trials. Use your history book, encyclopedia, and any other reference books to find some information about these trials. Write a brief description for as many of these questions, topics, names, or places as you can.

1. Dates of the Salem Witch Trials _____

2. Place/Colony where they took place _____

3. Religious group involved _____

4. What the colonists believed about witchcraft _____
   _____

5. How it all started _____
   _____

6. Who was Reverend Parris? _____

7. Who was Tituba? _____

8. What happened at the trials? _____

9. How many were accused? _____

10. How many were convicted? _____

11. How many were put to death? _____

12. From what you have read, why do you think these people persecuted those who were thought to be witches?

_____

_____

_____

_____

_____

_____

_____

Name _____

Basic Skills/U.S. History 6-8+

A FIGHT OVER LAND

Have you ever wondered who was fighting whom (and why) in the French & Indian War? Use reference books to help you fill in the blanks in this article with the terms on the left. By the time you finish, you'll be able to answer the questions who and why.

Louisbourg

General Braddock

William Pitt

Paris Treaty

Duquesne

Forks of the Ohio

Ontario

Iroquois

east

George Washington

Revolution

Quebec

Amherst

Necessity

Ticonderoga

Montcalm

Oswego

Britain

William Henry

militia

France and England both claimed the Forks of the Ohio River. Young ———— had been sent with troops to protect the
1
area for the British and to build a fort. But the French built Fort ———— right where Washington began building. When Wash-
2
ington built Fort ———— nearby, he was attacked by French &
3
Indian troops. Washington's small ———— was badly defeated.
4

The government in London sent a force of regulars under ———— to
5
defend British claims in the area. His army was soundly defeated near Fort Duquesne. The British then looked to the ———— League for assistance.
6
Other tribes, however, shifted allegiance to the French or claimed to be neutral in the struggle. In May 1756, ———— declared war on France.
7

Initially, the French forces lead by marquis de ———— won repeated
8
victories including the surrender of Fort ———— on Lake ———— . The
9   10
following year he destroyed Fort ———— , which was located at the south
11
end of Lake George.

Britain's new prime minister, ———— , increased aid to the American
12
colonies while French support was declining. As French supremacy began to come to an end, the British began gaining important victories led by Lord
———— . In 1758, the British forced the surrender of ———— and caused
13   14
the French to abandon the ———— . This victory led to the shift of tribal
15
support from the French to the British. ———— was the only major British
16
defeat during this period. In 1759, there were three major British successes: the taking of Niagara, the seizure of Ticonderoga and Crown Point, and Wolfe's defeat of Montcalm outside ———— . These events proved to be the begin-
17
ning of the end of French resistance in North America. Fighting finally ended with the British victory over the Cherokee in 1761.

The ———— gave Britain all lands of North America ———— of the
18   19
Mississippi River. The experience of the American colonists with the British regular forces had caused mutual dislike; the costly war had depleted the British treasury. These and other factors arising from the war helped set the stage for the ———— which followed in about 15 years.
20

Name _____

MIXED-UP REVOLUTIONARY EVENTS

The relationship between the colonies and the "mother" country, Britain, took a downhill turn after the French & Indian War. The British government wanted the colonies to pay for part of the cost of the war. In addition, the Parliament of England passed many other laws for the colonists to obey, without representation. This led to a "declaration of rights and grievances" and finally to full-scale military revolt. The events (below) from this period leading up to and through the Revolution are very mixed-up. Put them in chronological order by numbering them 1–20.

_____ Boston Tea Party   _____ First U.S. Submarine (Turtle)

_____ Constitutional Convention

_____ Battle of Trenton   _____ Ride of Dawes, Prescott, & Revere

_____ The Quartering Act   _____ Battle of Saratoga

_____ Declaration of Independence

_____ The Stamp Act   _____ The Boston Massacre

_____ Battle of Lexington and Concord

_____ Washington's Farewell Address   _____ Articles of Confederation

_____ Battle of Bunker Hill (Breed's Hill)

_____ First Continental Congress   _____ Washington crosses the Delaware

_____ Cornwallis surrenders at Yorktown   _____ Intolerable Acts

_____ The Treaty of Paris   _____ Winter at Valley Forge

THE 'REVERE'D RIDE

Name

MAPPING FREEDOM'S DOCUMENTS

Usually, you get a map when you need to see the location of places. You can also use a map to show ideas or diagram your thinking. This kind of map is sometimes called a "mind map." Below is the beginning of an idea map about a significant freedom document in American history. The Declaration of Independence was written by a committee appointed by the Continental Congress to declare independence from the British. The colonists were aware that to be successful every community must have laws to govern the behavior and interactions of its citizens both among themselves and with the outside world. Initially Americans were governed under a system referred to as a confederation. The Articles of Confederation were the first constitution. Later a new U.S. Constitution was written. Then the Bill of Rights was added to provide protection for citizens' liberties. From time to time, amendments are still added to the Constitution in order to address current problems.

Choose one of these four documents (The Declaration of Independence, The Articles of Confederation, The U.S. Constitution, or The Bill of Rights). Write its title in the large center box. Then create a mind map that summarizes the main features or provisions of the document, putting each item in one of the boxes. You can add more boxes where you need to.

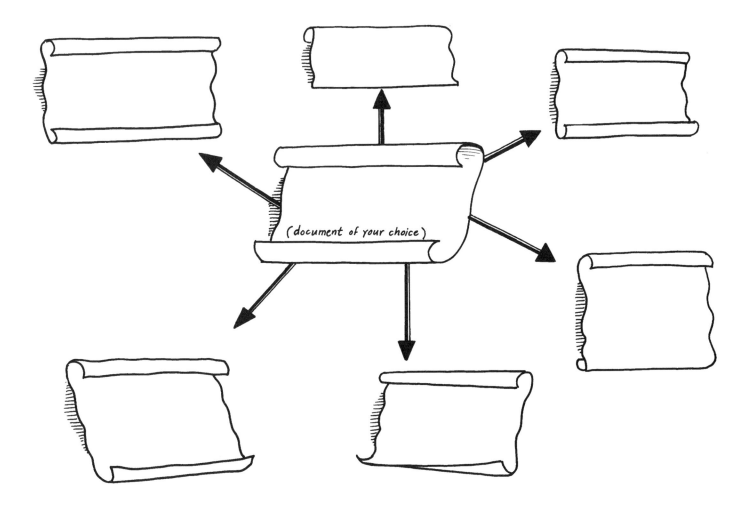

(document of your choice)

Name

A GREAT BARGAIN

Do you think 3¢ an acre is a good price for land? Someone did! Actually, this was the "asking price" of the French for the land they owned from New Orleans, up the Mississippi River, and west to the Rocky Mountains. Fill in the Louisiana outline map below with the answers to the six questions about this bargain purchase. Then answer the questions below the map.

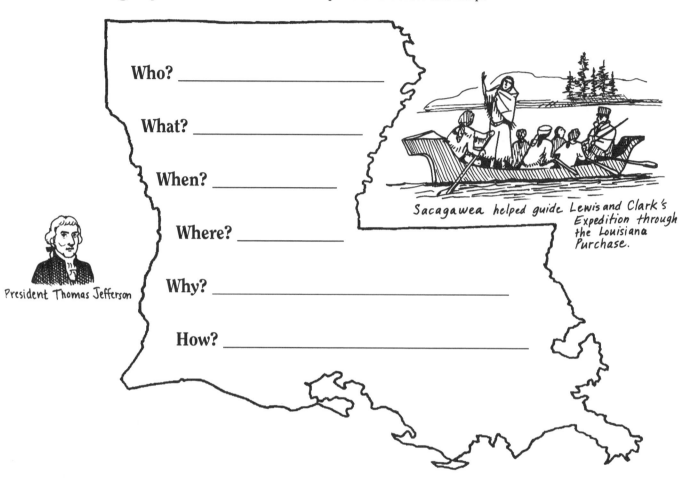

Who? _____

What? _____

When? _____

Where? _____

Why? _____

How? _____

President Thomas Jefferson

Sacagawea helped guide Lewis and Clark's Expedition through the Louisiana Purchase.

1. _____ owned this territory when the states signed the Constitution.

2. The Louisiana Purchase _____ the size of the U.S. and its territories.

3. Was the purchase of Louisiana a good deal for President Jefferson?

   Why or why not? _____

4. Why was Napoleon anxious to sell this territory? _____

5. What major port made the purchase important for the Americans and why? _____

Name _____

WAR, AGAIN!

By the winter of 1811, hostilities against Britain were rising again in the new country of the United States. These led to a war that produced some colorful heroes and long-remembered battles—the War of 1812. The words below feature some of the persons and events of this war. Match them with the clues 1–18. A word may be used more than once.

James Madison

Dolly Madison

neutrality

Great Britain

War Hawks

British Navy

Canada

Constitution

Washington

Chesapeake

France

American ships

"Old Ironsides"

"The Star
    Spangled
    Banner"

Battle of
    New Orleans

Andrew Jackson

1. became president in 1809 _____

2. countries at war with each other in Europe in 1809 _____

3. members of Congress who wanted war with Britain _____

4. principle of not taking sides in a war
   (James Madison encouraged this) _____

5. attacked by British at sea in early 1800s _____

6. U.S. sailors were kidnapped to serve here _____

7. country some congressmen believed
   was supplying Indians with guns _____

8. land War Hawks wanted to add to U.S. _____

9. country U.S. declared war on in June 1812 _____

10. where American attacks consistently failed _____

11. U.S. warship that sank the great British warship Guerriere _____

12. American warship captured by British, whose
    captain's last words were "Don't give up the ship!" _____

13. city burned by British in the war _____

14. nickname for the U.S.
    warship Constitution _____

15. poem written during the
    bombing of Ft. Henry _____
    _____

16. First Lady when the British
    attacked Washington in 1814
    _____

17. battle that took place after
    the war was actually ended
    _____

18. general who won victory at New Orleans
    _____

Name _____

WESTWARD, HO!

The late 1800s was a time of great growth in the United States. All that wide open country to the west just beckoned to people who wanted to farm, ranch, own land, and have adventures. Use the territorial expansion map and timeline on this page to help answer the following questions. Write your answers on another sheet of paper.

1803—Louisiana Purchase
1805—Lewis and Clark reach Pacific Ocean
1811—Cumberland Gap Road completed
1812—Oregon Trail, 2000 mile crossing
1819—Florida ceded by Spain
1821—Opening of the Santa Fe Trail
1823—Monroe Doctrine signed
1825—Erie Canal completed
1830—Congress passed Indian Removal Act
1836—Independence of Texas
1838—Cherokee Trail of Tears
1845—U.S. acquires Texas
1848—Ceded by Mexico
1853—Gadsden Purchase
1862—Homestead Act
1867—Purchase of Alaska
1869—Completion of first transcontinental railroad

1. What physical boundary originally prevented westward settlement? What historical event helped overcome this barrier?

2. Napoleon's financial problems led to the doubling of the physical territory of the U.S. What was this event called, and how did it aid western expansion?

3. Place these events in chronological order: Gadsden Purchase, Florida ceded by Spain, and area of upper midwest ceded by Great Britain.

4. What events led to the annexation of Texas by the U.S.?

5. Choose and trace two of the early trails across the U.S. frontier.

6. "54'40° or Fight" was a significant slogan during the acquisition of what territory? With whom was the dispute? How was this settled?

7. Trace the "Trail of Tears" on the map. What group of people were involved? Why was this event so named?

8. What current states were included in the area ceded by Mexico in 1848?

9. Place the following events in chronological order:
   ____ Erie Canal completed
   ____ Purchase of Alaska
   ____ Santa Fe Trail opened
   ____ First transcontinental railroad completed

Name _____

ABOLITION ARGUMENTS

While America was winning new territories, the argument over slavery divided the nation. The goal of anti-slavery groups was to prevent slavery from spreading. Some wanted to abolish slavery all together. The puzzle below presents some of the aspects of slavery and the fight for abolition. Use the clues to complete the puzzle.

Across

3. A plant raised to make blue dye
4. Famous novel that criticized slavery
8. The South threatened to _____ if the balance of free and slave states was not maintained.
9. The dream of every slave
11. John Brown raided Harper's Ferry for ____.
12. It was _____ to teach a slave to read or write.
17. Harriet _____, a runaway slave, led others to freedom.
18. A person who was forced to work on plantations
20. He filed a lawsuit for his freedom
22. Most important crop grown in the South in the 19th century
23. Slaves raised this crop in swampy areas.
24. Inventor of the cotton gin

Down

1. Frederick Douglass, a runaway slave, published a _____.
2. Freed female slave who became a powerful voice for female rights, _____ Truth
3. The strong agricultural economy of the South overshadowed the development of _____.
4. Road to freedom traveled by many slaves; _____ railroad
5. Kentucky senator known as the Great _____, Henry Clay
6. Laws passed by Southern states to control slaves
7. People who spoke out against slavery
10. National Anti-Slavery Society founder, Lucretia _____
13. This political party called for an end to slavery.
14. Slaves were legally classified as property or _____.
15. The majority of Southerners were small _____.
16. The number of slave states
19. African American preacher Nat _____ led slave revolt.
21. Novelist Harriet Beecher _____ criticized slavery.

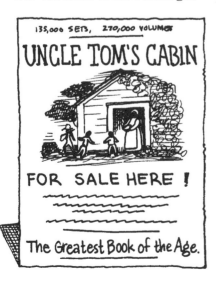

135,000 SETS, 270,000 VOLUMES

UNCLE TOM'S CABIN

FOR SALE HERE !

The Greatest Book of the Age.

Name

WHAT'S THE CONNECTION?

What event or situation during the Civil War period is connected to each of these headlines? Notice the dates, use references or your knowledge of the Civil War era, and write the answer below each headline.

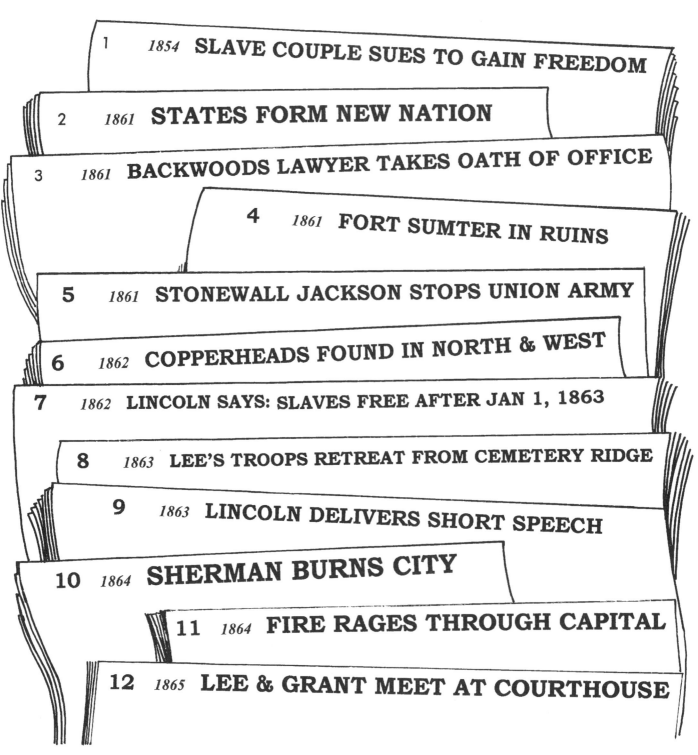

1 *1854* **SLAVE COUPLE SUES TO GAIN FREEDOM**

2 *1861* **STATES FORM NEW NATION**

3 *1861* **BACKWOODS LAWYER TAKES OATH OF OFFICE**

4 *1861* **FORT SUMTER IN RUINS**

5 *1861* **STONEWALL JACKSON STOPS UNION ARMY**

6 *1862* **COPPERHEADS FOUND IN NORTH & WEST**

7 *1862* **LINCOLN SAYS: SLAVES FREE AFTER JAN 1, 1863**

8 *1863* **LEE'S TROOPS RETREAT FROM CEMETERY RIDGE**

9 *1863* **LINCOLN DELIVERS SHORT SPEECH**

10 *1864* **SHERMAN BURNS CITY**

11 *1864* **FIRE RAGES THROUGH CAPITAL**

12 *1865* **LEE & GRANT MEET AT COURTHOUSE**

Name

TO REBUILD A NATION

Can you imagine what a nation would be like after a bitter war that killed many people, divided the rest of the people, and left terrible devastation? If, in addition, this war changed the whole structure of society, as the Civil War changed the American South, what would happen? The period from 1865-1877 was a critical time in the history of the United States as the country tried to rebuild.

Below are some of the building blocks; people, changes, and events that shaped Reconstruction. Give a brief description of each.

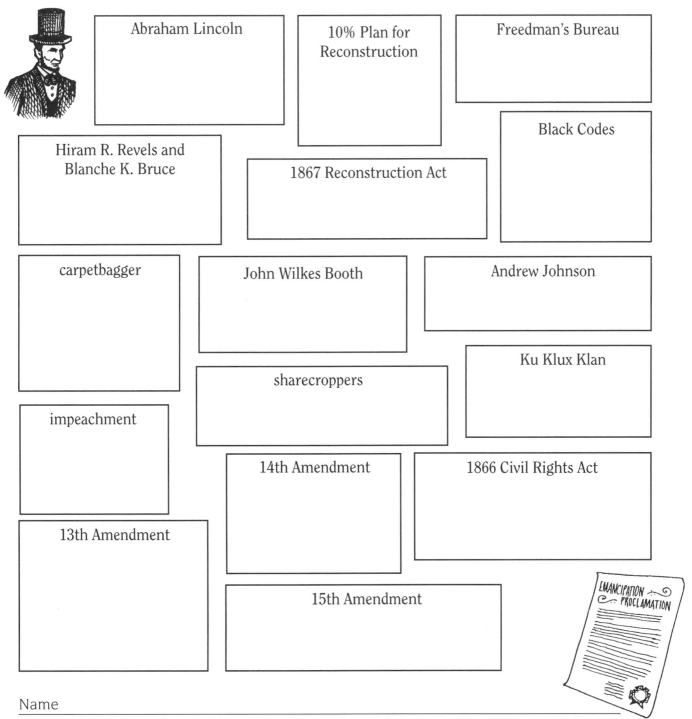

Abraham Lincoln

10% Plan for Reconstruction

Freedman's Bureau

Hiram R. Revels and Blanche K. Bruce

1867 Reconstruction Act

Black Codes

carpetbagger

John Wilkes Booth

Andrew Johnson

impeachment

sharecroppers

Ku Klux Klan

14th Amendment

1866 Civil Rights Act

13th Amendment

15th Amendment

Name

"FIFTY-FOUR FORTY OR FIGHT!"

This is a slogan from America's past. It was part of a concept called **manifest destiny**, that many Americans believed in by the 1840's. They thought the United States had the right and the duty to expand their rule from the Atlantic to the Pacific. This justified taking lands belonging to anyone considered inferior, such as the Native Americans and Mexicans. Manifest destiny was also the justification used for the Mexican War, the Spanish-American War, the annexation of Texas, and many other land acquisitions of the late nineteenth century. As the United States increased in size, it also increased as a world power. Find out about "fifty-four forty or fight" and other aspects of this period of time by filling in the blanks below.

1. "Fifty-four forty or fight" was the rallying cry of the Democrats who wanted to add the _____ Territory to the United States.

2. _____ was the land area purchased from the Russians in 1867.

3. The river that became the Texas/Mexico border is called the _____ .

4. The _____ Purchase from Mexico completed the 48 continental states.

5. _____ grants gave Americans permission to settle specific areas.

6. The Treaty of Guadalupe Hidalgo ended the _____ _____ .

7. The discovery of _____ increased the population of California, which was also called the Bear Flag Republic.

8. The Great Plains are bordered by the _____ River in the east and the _____ Mountains in the west.

9. The _____ were people who qualified for free government land.

10. The hammering of the "golden spike" at Promontory Point, Utah, in 1869 linked the Union Pacific and the Central Pacific to form the first _____ _____ .

11. Name four of the Indian nations of the Great Plains. _____ .

12. Native Americans were forced to live on limited areas of land called _____ .

13. As part of the peace treaty ending the Spanish-American War, _____ gained its freedom. Spain gave the U.S. _____ _____ in the Caribbean and _____ in the Pacific. The United States purchased the _____ for $20 million dollars.

14. _____ , annexed in 1898, is the only American state ever ruled by its own queen.

Name _____

INVENTORS & ROBBER BARONS

If TV talk shows had existed, the following men would probably have been on the guest lists. Match each man with his "claim to fame." (Find out what a "robber baron" is!)

_____

_____

_____

_____

_____

_____

_____

_____

_____

_____

_____

_____

_____

_____

_____

1. wrote a series of books featuring a poor boy who goes from "rags to riches"
2. coined the expression "The Four Hundred," meaning New York's socially elite
3. banker who founded U.S. Steel Company
4. controlled the oil industry and crushed the competition
5. inventor of the (adding) calculating machine
6. controlled and developed all aspects of the steel business and funded a library system
7. developed a process for changing iron into steel
8. developed the first incandescent electric bulb
9. perfected the first commercially useful telephone
10. invented the typewriter
11. built a one-cylinder gasoline engine
12. drilled the first oil well in Pennsylvania
13. the most powerful railroad baron of this period
14. drove the golden spike in the first transcontinental railroad
15. developed a way to send telegraph messages between moving railroad trains

HORATIO ALGER   WARD MCALLISTER   J. PIERPONT MORGAN

JOHN D. ROCKEFELLER   WILLIAM S. BURROUGHS   ANDREW CARNEGIE

HENRY BESSEMER & WILLIAM KELLY

THOMAS A. EDISON   ALEXANDER GRAHAM BELL   CHRISTOPHER SHOLES

J. FRANK DURYEA   EDWIN L. DRAKE   CORNELIUS VANDERBILT

LELAND STANFORD   GRANVILLE T. WOODS

Name _____

27

LABOR TRIVIA

In the mid-1860s, corporations were growing fast in America. As they grew, they gained great power over their labor force. This led to the growth of labor unions, which offered power and protection to workers. Match the number of the question about labor on each puzzle piece with the correct answer by placing the number in the correct blank. See if you can get all 15 matched correctly in 15 minutes.

_____ A. The process by which a third party settles a dispute by agreement of both labor and management.

_____ B. A single union represents all workers in a place of business.

_____ C. Negotiations by a union representative in the interest of union workers.

_____ D. An official complaint filed by a worker against management.

_____ E. The act of stepping in to settle a dispute.

_____ F. An owner locks out employees when management's terms are refused.

_____ G. Settling terms of exchange of wages and benefits for work.

_____ H. Union workers who stand outside a workplace to discourage the public from doing business with a company.

_____ I. Labor refuses to work until certain conditions are met.

_____ J. A person hired to do the work of a striker.

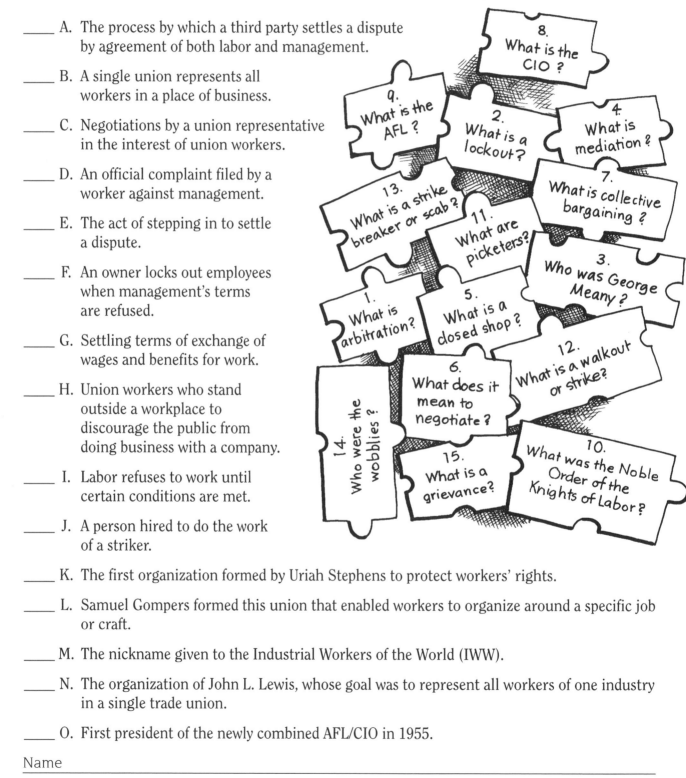

_____ K. The first organization formed by Uriah Stephens to protect workers' rights.

_____ L. Samuel Gompers formed this union that enabled workers to organize around a specific job or craft.

_____ M. The nickname given to the Industrial Workers of the World (IWW).

_____ N. The organization of John L. Lewis, whose goal was to represent all workers of one industry in a single trade union.

_____ O. First president of the newly combined AFL/CIO in 1955.

Name _____

THE WILD, WILD WEST

The "wild" west is most familiar to us in movies and TV shows. Cowboy adventures were only one part of the westward expansion and development. There was much more: the building of railroads, the Gold Rush, and the removal of the Native Americans were some of the major events of that period.

Look at the clues below. They all have to do with the Old West. Find the words in the puzzle to match the clues. (Look up, down, across, and diagonally. Words might be written backwards, too.)

1. folks who got free land to farm
2. railroad that joined the east and west
3. two railroad companies that built the transcontinental railroad
4. head of the Central Pacific Railroad
5. area set aside for Native Americans to live on
6. large nail used to build railroads
7. railroad spike driven into place in Utah on May 10, 1867
8. famous battle of Indian Wars in 1876
9. leaders of Sioux Indians in Battle of Little Bighorn
10. place in Colorado where gold was discovered in 1859

```
S  C  G  L  I  T  T  L  E  B  I  G  H  O  R  N
A  H  P  O  S  I  T  T  I  N  G  B  U  L  L  C
D  A  I  O  L  V  M  L  O  H  S  I  H  C  R  A
D  R  K  E  H  D  O  D  G  E  R  B  U  L  E  B
L  L  E  H  O  M  E  S  T  E  A  D  E  R  S  U
E  E  S  T  O  N  G  N  T  B  I  S  O  N  E  F
A  S  P  I  J  J  O  S  E  P  H  A  R  L  R  F
T  C  E  B  O  P  U  O  P  P  K  L  A  R  V  O
T  R  A  N  S  C  O  N  T  I  N  E  N  T  A  L
L  O  K  A  N  C  G  L  H  I  K  O  C  V  T  O
A  C  R  A  Z  Y  H  O  R  S  E  E  H  P  I  T
S  K  K  B  R  A  N  D  L  M  N  E  E  T  O  T
S  E  C  H  I  N  E  S  E  D  G  G  S  O  N  T
O  R  O  B  U  N  I  O  N  P  A  C  I  F  I  C
I  C  E  N  T  R  A  L  P  A  C  I  F  I  C  X
P  P  R  O  M  O  N  T  O  R  Y  P  O  I  N  T
```

Yee-ha!

11. place in Utah where last spike in the transcontinental railroad was driven
12. Union general in charge of Union Pacific Railroad, named Grenville _____
13. large areas of land used for raising cattle
14. reason many people went to California
15. mark put on cattle to show ownership
16. two names for large animals that roamed the Great Plains
17. route for driving herds of longhorn cattle from Texas to Abilene, Kansas for shipment by rail: _____ Trail
18. Nez Perce chief who marched a group of his people toward Canada
19. immigrants who helped build the transcontinental railroad
20. two belongings of cowboys

Name _____

THE GREAT WAR

It was called "The Great War" because never before had there been a war of this scope and size that involved so many countries. It was the largest war ever fought to that point in history. And the world hoped there would never be another one like it. Use the map on the next page and these activities to review some crucial information about World War I.

1. Look at the map on page 31 and use your history book or encyclopedia to find the countries that were part of the **Allied Powers** during the war. Write their names below. There are sixteen. Shade these countries green on the map. Two Allies are not shown on this map because they are not in the European area. Be sure to include them on the list.

2. Write the names of the countries in the **Axis (Central) Powers** (below). There are four. Shade these countries yellow on the map.

3. Also write the names of the countries in Europe that were neutral. Shade them purple.

Allied Powers	Central (Axis) Powers	Neutral Countries

4. Locate and label in red the spot where Germany sank the British passenger ship, *Lusitania*, off the southern coast of Ireland. This ship was carrying many Americans, and this was the event that finally drew the United States into the war.

5. List below three or more **causes** of the war and three or more **effects** of the war.

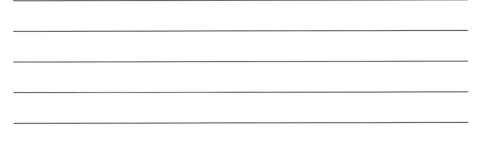

Use with page 31.

Name _____

Use with page 30.

WORLD WAR I MAP

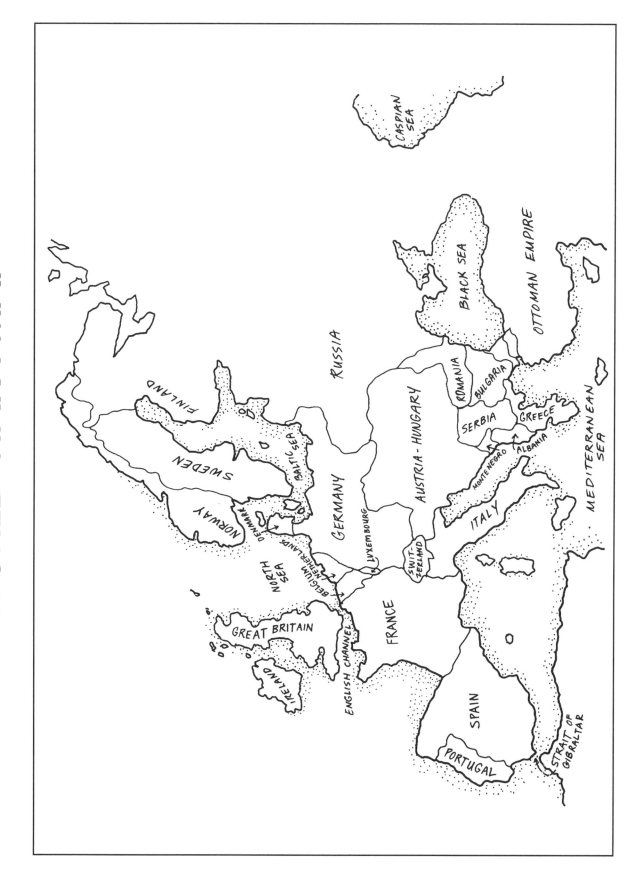

Name

THE DECADE THAT ROARED

In January 1920, *Life Magazine* summarized the mood of Americans following the end of the "war to end all wars."

> *"Forget about the war, seems to be the slogan of the American people just at present. Spend; travel; dine, jazz, dash off to Florida, to California, to Europe, anywhere, everywhere; buy expensive automobiles, luxurious houses, costly jewelry; throw money right and left, but— forget about the war."*

During the 1920s older Americans became concerned about the way the country was changing. Teenagers and young adults shocked their parents by doing wild dances, listening to new forms of music, wearing strange clothes, and speaking in a "strange" language. This was also the decade of many new inventions—radios, movies, automobiles, electric refrigerators, and vacuum cleaners. It was indeed a fascinating decade—squeezed between two tough periods—the Great War and the Great Depression. Search around in some reference books to find out about five of the 1920s people, places, inventions, or events shown below. Write a brief description or explanation about the items you choose.

THE COTTON CLUB   THE HARLEM RENAISSANCE   DUKE ELLINGTON

CAB CALLOWAY   JAZZ   MARIAN ANDERSON

THE TEAPOT DOME SCANDAL

PRESIDENT HARDING   PRESIDENT COOLIDGE   THE LEAGUE OF NATIONS

THE AMERICAN FOOTBALL ASSOCIATION

HENRY FORD'S MODEL T   PROHIBITION   LOUIS ARMSTRONG

CHARLES LINDBERGH   BABE RUTH

RADIO BROADCASTING   STOCK MARKET   THE NEW WOMAN

MOTION PICTURES   SWING DANCING   JACK DEMPSEY

HARLEM GLOBETROTTERS

GERTRUDE EDERLE   ERNEST HEMINGWAY   GERTRUDE STEIN

WILLIAM FAULKNER   FLAPPERS   KNUTE ROCKNE

_____

_____

_____

_____

_____

_____

Name _____

HEY BUDDY, CAN YOU SPARE A DIME?

By August 1929, some major investors had begun selling their stocks and buying government savings bonds instead. The rash of selling caused stock prices to fall. On Tuesday, October 29, a stampede of selling hit the New York Stock Exchange. Fortunes were "wiped out" in a single day. Following the stock market crash, the economy slid into a severe depression. People literally were in need of a dime!

Use the clues to complete the puzzle of information about this event in U.S. history.

1. U.S. monetary system went off this standard during the Depression.

2. October 29, 1929, marked the stock market _____ .

3. President during early depression told people this was "just around the corner."

4. Many farmers were forced to leave their land due to defaults on mortgage payments, and became _____ workers, moving in search of work.

5. Nickname given to October 29, 1929, the day of the stock market crash.

6. New president in 1932 (initials)

7. President Roosevelt's Plan for economic recovery.

8. The Depression brought job loss and high rates of _____ .

9. People blamed President Hoover for the shanty towns (which were referred to as _____) that grew up around cities.

10. Level of government that people expected to cure the economic ills.

11. The march on Washington by a group of World War I veterans demanding payment of their war bonus.

12. Farmers suffered not only from the economic depression but also from a ten-year drought that created the _____ .

13. People sought food and relief in bread lines or in _____ .

14. President who had little success with the economic troubles.

15. The rush to take savings from banks; known as the Great _____ .

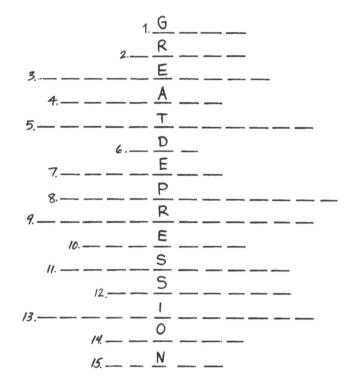

```
1.  G _ _ _ _
2. _ R _ _ _
3. _ _ _ _ E _ _ _ _
4. _ _ _ A _ _ _
5. _ _ _ _ _ T _ _ _ _ _ _
6. _ _ D _
7. _ _ _ _ E _ _
8. _ _ _ _ P _ _ _ _ _ _ _ _
9. _ _ _ _ R _ _ _ _
10. _ _ _ E _ _ _
11. _ _ _ _ S _
12. _ _ _ S _ _ _ _
13. _ _ _ _ I _ _ _ _
14. _ _ _ O _ _ _
15. _ _ N _ _ _
```

WAS THE NEW DEAL A GOOD DEAL?

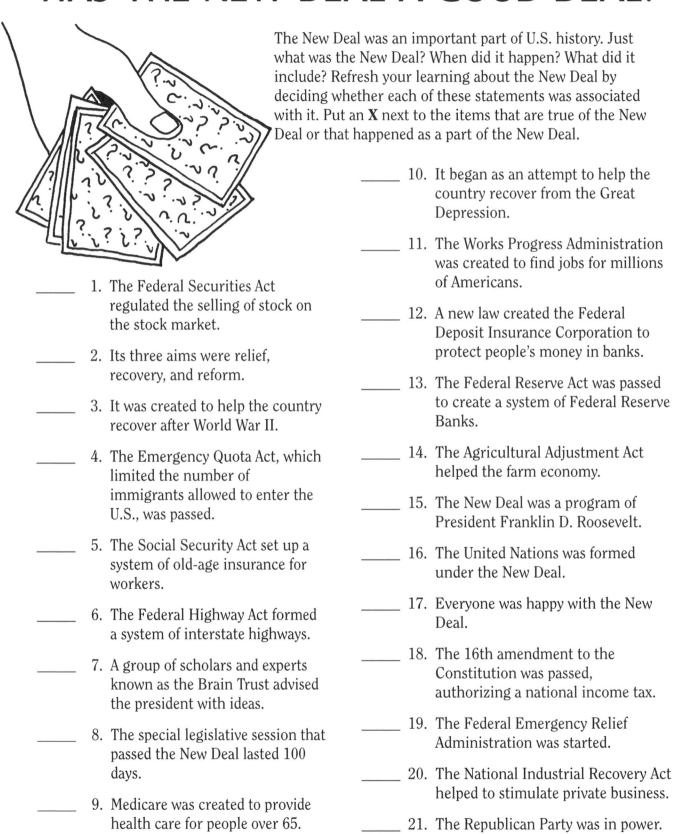

The New Deal was an important part of U.S. history. Just what was the New Deal? When did it happen? What did it include? Refresh your learning about the New Deal by deciding whether each of these statements was associated with it. Put an **X** next to the items that are true of the New Deal or that happened as a part of the New Deal.

_____ 1. The Federal Securities Act regulated the selling of stock on the stock market.

_____ 2. Its three aims were relief, recovery, and reform.

_____ 3. It was created to help the country recover after World War II.

_____ 4. The Emergency Quota Act, which limited the number of immigrants allowed to enter the U.S., was passed.

_____ 5. The Social Security Act set up a system of old-age insurance for workers.

_____ 6. The Federal Highway Act formed a system of interstate highways.

_____ 7. A group of scholars and experts known as the Brain Trust advised the president with ideas.

_____ 8. The special legislative session that passed the New Deal lasted 100 days.

_____ 9. Medicare was created to provide health care for people over 65.

_____ 10. It began as an attempt to help the country recover from the Great Depression.

_____ 11. The Works Progress Administration was created to find jobs for millions of Americans.

_____ 12. A new law created the Federal Deposit Insurance Corporation to protect people's money in banks.

_____ 13. The Federal Reserve Act was passed to create a system of Federal Reserve Banks.

_____ 14. The Agricultural Adjustment Act helped the farm economy.

_____ 15. The New Deal was a program of President Franklin D. Roosevelt.

_____ 16. The United Nations was formed under the New Deal.

_____ 17. Everyone was happy with the New Deal.

_____ 18. The 16th amendment to the Constitution was passed, authorizing a national income tax.

_____ 19. The Federal Emergency Relief Administration was started.

_____ 20. The National Industrial Recovery Act helped to stimulate private business.

_____ 21. The Republican Party was in power.

Name _____

THE BIG ONE

Look at the jumbled list of important events related to World War II. Your task is to determine the chronological order of events and arrange them on the timeline. (Write a shortened version of the event along the timeline.) You'll need references to find the dates.

Hitler occupies Czechoslovakia.

Invasion of Italy begins.

France surrenders to Germany.

The British Navy sinks the German warship *Bismarck*.

Japan signs surrender.

Britain and France declare war on Germany;
   U.S. remains neutral.

Battle of Britain begins.

Soviet Union announces its neutrality.

U.S. drops atomic bomb on Hiroshima, Japan.

Allies win battle of Midway in the South Pacific.

Allied troops land in Algeria and Morocco.

Allies capture Tarawa Island in the Pacific.

Japan bombs Pearl Harbor, Hawaii.

U.S. declares war on Japan.

Roosevelt and Churchill meet in U.S.

Germany surrenders.

Germany and Italy declare war on the U.S.

Battle of the Bulge ends.

U.S. victory in Solomon Islands.

U.S. captures Nuremberg, Germany.

Allies capture Naples, Italy.

U.S. drops atomic bomb on Nagasaki, Japan.

U.S. captures Okinawa in Pacific.

Paris, France, is liberated by Allies.

President Roosevelt dies; Truman becomes
   president of the U.S.

U.S. marines capture Iwo Jima.

1939

1940

1941

1942

1943

1944

1945

Name

OUT OF THE RUINS

The end of World War II saw much of Europe and Asia in ruins. While the war did not affect the United States physically, much of the economy was tied to the war effort, shortages of goods were widespread, and the influx of returning GIs and their young families strained the housing market. In the early postwar years, returning veterans were faced with a lack of jobs and educational opportunities. But as the postwar years progressed, economic growth and prosperity brought Americans to the highest standard of living ever enjoyed by any society. The following pairs of statements describe some events in the postwar years. For each pair, decide which is the cause (C) and which is the effect (E). Write the correct letter before each sentence.

1. ____ Much of Europe was devastated by World War II.

____ The Marshall Plan was a long-range plan of recovery from the war.

2. ____ The GI Bill of Rights was passed to help veterans buy homes and attend school.

____ Many veterans' educations were cut short by wartime service.

3. ____ Farmers increased the use of dangerous pesticides.

____ Rachel Carson publishes *Silent Spring,* a call to protect the environment.

4. ____ Dr. Jonas Salk introduces the polio vaccine to American school children.

____ Polio, a contagious disease, limits children's use of parks and pools.

5. ____ Migrant farm laborers' working conditions are deplorable.

____ Cesar Chavez founds the National Farm Workers Association in California.

6. ____ The Soviet Union launches the first satellite, *Sputnik.*

____ The United States gears up its space program.

7. ____ The United Nations was formed in 1945 to maintain world peace and security.

____ There was a need for an impartial international cooperation to preserve peace.

8. ____ Lyndon B. Johnson becomes the thirty-sixth president of the United States.

____ President John F. Kennedy is assassinated in Dallas, Texas.

9. ____ U.S. troops are sent to Little Rock, Arkansas, to enforce school desegregation.

____ The Supreme Court rules in favor of Brown in the case *Brown vs. Board of Education.*

10. ____ The U.S., France, and Great Britain announced plans in 1948 to create an independent Republic of West Germany.

____ The Soviets closed all roads leading across their zone of Berlin.

11. ____ The U.S., France, and Great Britain airlifted supplies into West Berlin.

____ The Soviets closed all roads leading across their zone of Berlin.

Name

FROM YALTA TO THE FALL OF THE WALL

In 1947, financier Bernard Baruch stated, "We are in the midst of a cold war." When countries choose to fight with words, not guns, they are said to be engaging in a cold war. The Cold War was a struggle between democratic nations of the West and the nations allied with what was then called the Soviet Union. The Cold War Period lasted from the Yalta Convention at the close of World War II until the fall of the Berlin Wall in 1989.

Find ten events, persons, or policies from the Cold War. Briefly describe them in the spaces below—in the sequence they occurred. Include dates. Some ideas are given to get you started on your research.

Yalta Convention
22nd Amendment
puppet government
communism
capitalism
McCarthyism
Korean War
Truman Doctrine
Marshall Plan
Bay of Pigs
Eisenhower
satellite nations
NATO
Warsaw Pact
Nixon
Berlin Blockade
Kennedy
Iron Curtain
Henry Kissinger
Chinese Civil War
nuclear weapons
John Foster Dulles
summit
U-2 Affair
McCarthy Hearings
Cuban Revolution
Berlin Wall
Sputnik
Nikita Khrushchev
containment
Vietnam

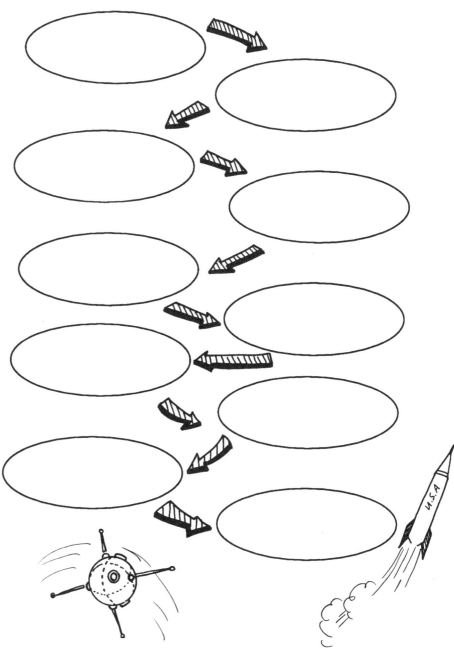

Name

A COUNTRY DIVIDED

Korea was liberated from Japanese occupation by a joint Soviet–U.S. invasion force during World War II. The peninsula was divided at the **38th parallel** with the Soviets controlling **the northern half** and the U.S. controlling **the southern half.** At the end of the war, neither power would release its half so Korea remained divided. Both Korean governments claimed the right to rule all of Korea. When northern forces invaded the south on June 25, 1950, the UN Security Council accepted an American request for immediate aid to South Korea. Because the Soviet delegate was absent at the time of the vote, the resolution was passed. More than a dozen members joined with the U.S. in defending South Korea.

In June of 1950, North Korea crossed the 38th parallel and pushed South Korean and American forces back to the area around Pusan on the southeast coast. In September of 1950, American General Douglas MacArthur led an expeditionary force that landed behind enemy lines at **Inchon** on the northwest coast of South Korea. The North Koreans were pushed back across the 38th parallel almost to the **Yalu River** which separates Korea and the People's Republic of China. When the Chinese received no reply to their diplomatic efforts to have UN troops leave the border region, they charged across the border. They rapidly drove UN troops back across the 38th parallel. This battle line was roughly the same as the old north-south boundary between the two Koreas.

After two years of negotiations, an armistice was finally reached in 1953. The city of **Panmunjom** is located on the border and has been the site of many negotiations between **Seoul** and **P'yongyang.** The war cost many American lives and created a rift between President Harry Truman and General Douglas MacArthur that helped General Dwight D. Eisenhower win the presidential election of 1950.

Sketch the Korean peninsula. Locate and label all of the important geographic sites mentioned above. Label all surrounding bodies of water and the countries that share a border with North Korea.

Name

THE 60s: A TIME OF TURMOIL

During the 1960s, the U.S. became involved in many serious social, cultural, and political crises. The age of assassinations, Civil Rights, and Vietnam also produced many advances in science and social issues. The crossword puzzle below includes some aspects of the sixties. Use the clues to complete the puzzle.

Across

3. Nixon and Kennedy were the first presidential candidates to _____ on television.
4. President Kennedy's peace army became the Peace _____ .
5. President Lyndon Johnson proposed the _____ Society.
9. Disastrous CIA-backed invasion of Cuba's _____ _____ _____ .
10. Native Americans demanded the government honor treaty obligations made at _____ Knee.
11. Largest rock concert of the 1960s was _____ .
14. National Organization for Women is also known as _____ .
15. Federal medical aid to the elderly is called _____ .
16. Muhammed Ali was formerly known as Cassius _____ .
17. The Civil _____ Act of 1964 outlawed discrimination against African Americans and women workers.
18. In 1969 Neil _____ was the first to step on the moon.
19. What did Lee Harvey Oswald, Sirhan Sirhan, and James Earl Ray have in common?

Down

1. John F. _____ was inaugurated President in 1960.
2. The most committed members of the counterculture were known as _____ .
6. Confrontation between Russia and U.S. over missile placement was the Cuban _____ _____ .
7. A group of people living together and providing for their own needs is called a _____ .
8. University in Ohio where several student demonstrators were killed was _____ State.
9. Cesar Chavez organized a _____ against grapes and lettuce to unionize migrant workers.
12. Southeast Asian country to which American troops were sent as advisors.
13. During the 1963 March on Washington, Martin Luther _____ , Jr. gave his famous speech.
16. _____ fled to the U.S. to escape Castro's rule.

Name _____

A LONG TIME IN VIETNAM

The timeline below records the major events of the U.S. involvement in Vietnam. As you read through the timeline, you will notice key words have been omitted.
Write the omitted word(s) on the blank provided.

1954 ————— 1. U.S. sends _____ aid to South Vietnam.

1959 ————— 2. First two U.S. soldiers _____ in Vietnam.

1961 ————— 3. President _____ sends military advisors to South Vietnam.

1964 ————— 4. President _____ elected to a full term.

————— 5. President persuades Congress to pass a resolution to send thousands of U.S. _____ to Vietnam.
—— Gulf of Tonkin Resolution passed.
—— President Johnson orders the bombing of North Vietnam.

1967 ————— 6. Tet (Vietnamese lunar New Year) Offensive; North Vietnam launches a campaign attacking the U.S. Embassy in _____ .

1968 ————— 540,000 American troops on duty in Vietnam.
—— Peace talks begin between the U.S. and Vietnam.

————— 7. President _____ promises to withdraw troops from Vietnam.

1969 ————— 8. Anti-Vietnam War _____ hold their largest rally in Washington, D.C.
—— 9. Nixon orders bombing of Communist bases in _____ .

1970 ————— 10. National Guard fires on antiwar demonstration at _____ University; 4 students die.
—— Nixon brings home 150,000 troops from Vietnam.

1973 ————— Fighting ceases in Vietnam War.

————— 11. Henry Kissinger of the U.S. and Le Duc Tho of North Vietnam awarded the Nobel _____ Prize for negotiating a cease fire.
—— U.S. troops withdraw from Vietnam.

1975 ————— South Vietnam falls to Communist forces.

————— 12. _____ wins the civil war in Cambodia, renaming the country Kampuchea.

Name _____

THE GREAT SPACE RACE

Russia launched the first artificial satellite in 1957. The first successful U.S. launch, *Explorer I,* occurred the following year. By 1962, both the United States and the Soviet Union had launched astronauts into space. By the end of the decade Americans had landed on the moon.

The answer to each of the questions below is included in the word search. Fill in each blank, and circle the words in the puzzle.

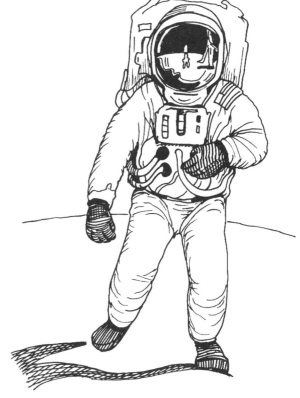

```
F  A  R  M  S  T  R  O  N  G  M  Y  A  G
W  F  E  N  P  K  D  A  S  A  N  T  N  B
M  I  O  B  O  W  K  N  M  X  I  I  S  E
H  K  A  T  O  P  F  B  E  B  K  C  P  Q
E  N  Q  S  F  R  X  C  R  C  H  L  U  T
T  B  Q  R  T  I  P  O  O  M  A  N  T  I
I  N  O  Q  L  R  L  D  L  V  S  N  N  Y
L  N  U  R  F  S  O  L  K  X  V  R  I  R
L  O  D  K  C  O  E  N  V  Q  B  Y  K  T
E  O  U  R  L  N  P  S  A  N  P  M  X  N
T  M  U  L  G  I  C  D  Q  U  N  E  Q  E
A  B  O  E  X  W  J  H  C  S  T  E  G  E
S  P  R  U  M  J  T  R  D  A  P  S  L  R
A  C  O  S  M  O  N  A  U  T  I  L  N  G
```

WORD SEARCH CLUES

1. Another name for space explorers is _____.
2. The first extraterrestrial landing was on the _____ .
3. To cancel a mission is to _____.
4. _____ was the space shuttle that exploded in 1986.
5. The first man to step on the moon was Neil _____ .
6. _____ is the name given to a Russian astronaut.
7. The first man-made satellite to orbit Earth was _____ .
8. _____ is the path of one body around another.
9. A man-made object intended to orbit a celestial body is a _____.
10. Craft with recording instruments that moves through space is a _____ .
11. Bringing two spacecrafts together in space is called _____.
12. _____ is the time at which the spacecraft leaves the launch pad.
13. Returning to Earth through the atmosphere is called _____ .
14. The area from which a rocket is launched is the _____ .
15. The first American to orbit Earth was John _____.
16. The _____ project landed the first man on the moon.
17. The abbreviation for National Aeronautics & Space Administration is _____ .

Name _____

PRESIDENTIAL PARADE

Who were the presidents of the United States? Finish this timeline of American presidents by writing the name and dates of each presidency. You may use an encyclopedia, history textbook, or any other references.

Name

Basic Skills/U.S. History 6-8+ Copyright ©1997 by Incentive Publications, Inc., Nashville, TN.

CHAMPIONS, PIONEERS, & FIRST LADIES

There are many famous American men, but there are also many famous American women you should know. Match the clues with names of American women.

____ CLARA BARTON

____ SACAGAWEA

____ SANDRA DAY O'CONNOR

____ FLORENCE GRIFFITH JOYNER

____ ROSA PARKS

____ LOUISA MAY ALCOTT

____ HARRIET TUBMAN

____ CORETTA SCOTT KING

____ RUTH GINSBERG

____ ELEANOR ROOSEVELT

____ SALLY RIDE

____ HELEN KELLER

____ HARRIET BEECHER STOWE

____ WILMA MANKILLER

____ LILIUOKALANI

____ GERALDINE FERRARO

____ AMELIA EARHART

____ ROSALYN SUSSMAN YALOW

1. Guided Lewis and Clark on their exploration of the West

2. Known as "Moses" because she led her people out of slavery

3. After her husband's death, became a prominent voice in the Civil Rights movement

4. Perhaps the most influential, most criticized, and most revered of all First Ladies

5. An example of hope for people with severe disabilities

6. First woman to serve as Principal Chief of the Cherokee Nation

7. America's only native born queen

8. First U.S. female astronaut in space

9. First woman appointed to U.S. Supreme Court

10. First woman to fly solo across the Atlantic

11. Became the second woman ever to win the Nobel Prize in medicine

12. Author of *Little Women*

13. First female U.S. vice-presidential candidate

14. African-American woman who refused to yield her seat on a bus

15. Woman who founded the American Red Cross

16. Writer of *Uncle Tom's Cabin,* influential novel about slavery

17. Second woman appointed to U.S. Supreme Court

18. Gold-medal-winning U.S. track and field star

Name _____

TOWARD CIVIL RIGHTS

As you read the following paragraphs about the Civil Rights Movement, fill in the blanks with the appropriate word(s) from the Word Bank below.

WORD BANK

Eisenhower	deprive	Montgomery	unconstitutional
liberty	voice	discrimination	segregating
clergyman	citizenship	Rosa Parks	guaranteed
Johnson	integration	Robinson	Civil Rights

The Civil Rights Act of 1866 gave citizenship to African Americans. The Republican Congress overrode the veto of President ——— 1 . The Republicans were afraid that the Supreme Court might declare the Civil Rights Act ——— 2 . They, therefore, proposed the Fourteenth Amendment to the Constitution which granted ——— 3 to all persons born or naturalized in the United States. It also ——— 4 "equal protection of the laws" for all citizens and declared that no state could " ——— 5 any person of life, ——— 6 , or property without due process of law."

In 1869 the Fifteenth Amendment was proposed by Republicans in Congress. It forbade any state to deny any American male over twenty-one the right to vote. ——— 7 continued, however, especially in the areas of housing, employment, education, and the military, and through the Jim Crow Laws in the South and poll taxes.

Jackie ——— 8 became the first African American to play professional baseball when he signed a contract in 1947 to play with the Brooklyn Dodgers. In 1948, President Truman ordered the military to cease ——— 9 blacks into separate units. The Supreme Court in 1954 ruled in favor of Brown in the case *Brown vs. Board of Education of Topeka* which stated that separate schools could never be equal. In 1957, Central High School in Little Rock, Arkansas, became the focus for school ——— 10 when Governor Orval Faubus called out the National Guard. President ——— 11 sent troops to Little Rock because the Governor was defying federal law. ——— 12 , a member of the NAACP, brought attention to Alabama's Jim Crow Laws in 1955 when she was arrested for refusing to give up her bus seat to a white man. This event triggered the ——— 13 bus boycott . . . "asking every Negro to stay off the buses on Monday in protest of the arrest and trial." A young black ——— 14 , the Reverend Martin Luther King, Jr., an early supporter of the boycott, was already becoming the most powerful ——— 15 in the Civil Rights Movement. During the 1960s, the Civil Rights Movement grew and spread to encompass not only African Americans but also Native Americans, Asian Americans, Latinos, women, disabled persons, and other minority groups.

Name

WHO SAID THAT?

These are some of the most repeated, quoted, and recorded statements in American history. But who said them? See if you can recognize the speakers and match the quotations with them. (Write the letter next to each quotation.)

_____ 1. The British are coming! The British are coming!

_____ 2. I know not what course others may take; but as for me, give me liberty or give me death.

_____ 3. There, I guess King George will be able to read that.

_____ 4. I have not yet begun to fight.

_____ 5. I only regret that I have but one life to lose for my country.

_____ 6. You must obey this now—for a law—that he who will not work shall not eat.

_____ 7. If slavery must go by blood and war, let war come.

_____ 8. Go west, young man; go west!

_____ 9. We are in the midst of a cold war.

_____ 10. That's one small step for man, one giant leap for mankind.

_____ 11. If Lincoln were alive today, he would be spinning in his grave.

_____ 12. You shall not crucify mankind upon a cross of gold.

_____ 13. The only thing we have to fear is fear itself.

_____ 14. Speak softly and carry a big stick.

_____ 15. You have to be able to take a lot of criticism—suffer defeats, and get up tomorrow and fight again.

_____ 16. Ask not what your country can do for you. Ask what you can do for your country.

_____ 17. . . . thank God Almighty we are free, free at last.

_____ 18. Old soldiers never die, they just fade away.

A. Nathan Hale

B. John F. Kennedy

C. Neil Armstrong

D. William Jennings Bryant

E. Paul Revere

F. John Quincy Adams

G. Franklin D. Roosevelt

H. John Hancock

I. Captain John Smith

J. Gen. Douglas MacArthur

K. Patrick Henry

L. Gerald Ford

M. Theodore Roosevelt

N. John Quincy Adams

O. John Paul Jones

P. Martin Luther King, Jr.

Q. Bernard Baruch

R. Bill Clinton

S. Horace Greeley

Name _____

FAMOUS PLACES & SPACES

The United States is rich with historic landmarks and monuments. One aspect of citizenship in a country is knowing about its past, its traditions, and its historic treasures. Listed below are some major geographic features, historical sites, monuments, or significant institutions from each of the fifty states. On the map on the following page, write the number found beside each set of features in the state where these are found.

Travel America!

1. Princeton University, located at the site of a Revolutionary War Battle
2. Columbia River Gorge and Mt. Hood
3. The Grand Ole Opry and the Hermitage
4. Battle of Gettysburg and Liberty Bell
5. Cajun country famous for Mardi Gras
6. Redstone Arsenal and Space and Rocket Museum
7. Pearl Harbor and Kilauea Volcano
8. 15,000 lakes and the Mayo Clinic
9. Mammoth Cave and Churchill Downs
10. Fort Sumter, site of the first shots of the Civil War
11. Majority of Yellowstone National Park and the Grand Teton Mountains
12. Home state of 8 U.S. presidents and Kings Island
13. Location of Plymouth Rock and Salem Trials
14. The oldest U.S. city and site of the Everglades
15. Pikes Peak, Cave of the Winds, Mesa Verde
16. Lewis and Clark State Park, Herbert Hoover's home state
17. Atomic research occurs at both White Sands and Los Alamos
18. Home of Hot Springs and Ozark Mountains
19. Arcadia National Park, the only national park in New England
20. Jamestown settlement and Battle of York Town
21. Brandywine Creek State Park and the home of Du Pont Family
22. Lake Mead, Hoover Dam, and Mohave Desert
23. Theodore Roosevelt National Park in the Badlands and the Red River Valley
24. Lincoln's Log Cabin and Sears Tower
25. Denali Mountain Peak and Klondike Park
26. The Alamo and Rio Grande
27. Camp David and U.S. Naval Academy

visit historic landmarks and monuments

28. Will Rogers Memorial, Fort Sill and Native American tribes call it home
29. Okefenokee Swamp and Stone Mountain
30. Painted Desert and the Grand Canyon
31. Nathan Hale Homestead
32. Death Valley and Redwood Forest
33. Dodge City and Eisenhower Birthplace
34. Green Bay and Lake Winnebago
35. Vicksburg National Military Park and Rosemont Plantation, last home of Confederate President Jefferson Davis
36. Sun Valley and Soda Springs Geyser
37. Kitty Hawk and Biltmore House
38. Indianapolis 500 and Notre Dame
39. Mount Rainier, Mount St. Helens, and the Space Needle
40. Green Mountains and Ft. Ticonderoga
41. Henry Ford and Motown Museums
42. Newport and Gen. Nathanael Greene's home
43. Little Bighorn Battlefield and parts of Glacier National Park
44. Harper's Ferry National Historical Park and Wheeling Suspension Bridge
45. Empire State Building and Niagara Falls
46. The birthplace of Harry S. Truman and the Gateway Arch
47. The Mormon Temple and the Great Salt Lake
48. Mt. Rushmore, Wounded Knee Monument, and the Badlands
49. Mt. Washington, Lake Winnipesaukee, and Christa McAuliffe Planetarium
50. Homestead National Monument, birthplace of Gerald Ford, and Boys Town

Use with page 47.

Name

Use with page 46.

UNITED STATES MAP

MAINE
MASSACHUSETTS
RHODE ISLAND
CONNECTICUT
NEW JERSEY
DELAWARE
MARYLAND
NEW HAMPSHIRE
VERMONT
NEW YORK
PENNSYLVANIA
VIRGINIA
N. CAROLINA
S. CAROLINA
FLORIDA
OHIO
W. VIRGINIA
KENTUCKY
TENNESSEE
GEORGIA
ALABAMA
MISSISSIPPI
MICHIGAN
INDIANA
ILLINOIS
MISSOURI
ARKANSAS
LOUISIANA
WISCONSIN
IOWA
MINNESOTA
N. DAKOTA
S. DAKOTA
NEBRASKA
KANSAS
OKLAHOMA
TEXAS
COLORADO
NEW MEXICO
MONTANA
WYOMING
UTAH
ARIZONA
IDAHO
NEVADA
CALIFORNIA
WASHINGTON
OREGON
HAWAII
ALASKA

Name

INVENTIONS & INVENTORS

Are you aware that Americans are known for their inventiveness? No matter how far back in American history you go, the sense of creativity is evident. The puzzle below presents some of America's greatest inventors. The names of the inventors are the clues. The puzzle words are the names of their inventions.

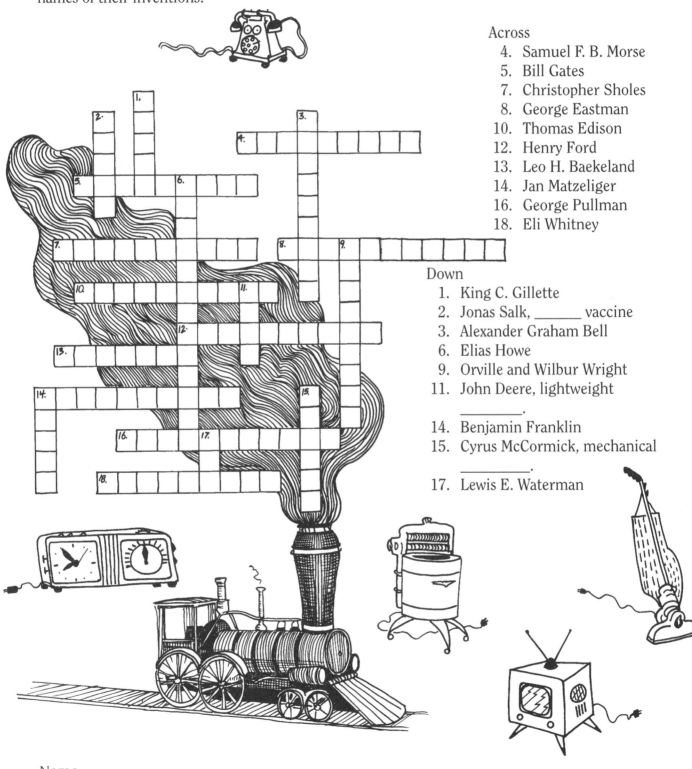

Across
  4. Samuel F. B. Morse
  5. Bill Gates
  7. Christopher Sholes
  8. George Eastman
  10. Thomas Edison
  12. Henry Ford
  13. Leo H. Baekeland
  14. Jan Matzeliger
  16. George Pullman
  18. Eli Whitney

Down
  1. King C. Gillette
  2. Jonas Salk, _____ vaccine
  3. Alexander Graham Bell
  6. Elias Howe
  9. Orville and Wilbur Wright
  11. John Deere, lightweight
    _____.
  14. Benjamin Franklin
  15. Cyrus McCormick, mechanical
    _____.
  17. Lewis E. Waterman

Name _____

APPENDIX

CONTENTS

GLOSSARY OF U.S. HISTORY TERMS

abolitionist: person who wanted to end slavery in the U.S.

AFL-CIO: labor union organization formed by the merger in 1955 of two powerful unions

Allies: an alliance of nations that fought together in World War I and World War II

amendment: a change or addition to a law

amnesty: official pardon for a crime committed against the government

antiwar movement: a campaign to end a war; particularly the Vietnam War in the U.S.

Appomattox: Virginia courthouse where Lee surrendered to Grant at the end of the Civil War

Articles of Confederation: the agreement in which the thirteen original colonies established a government

Atlantic Charter: 1941 agreement in which U.S. and Great Britain pledged to work for a war-free world

Bacon's Rebellion: the revolt of Virginia colonists 1676

balance of power: equal military and economic strength between two or more nations

Battle of Bunker Hill: the first major battle of the Revolutionary War

Battle of Gettysburg: 1863, Union forces defeated Lee's invasion of the North

Battle of New Orleans: a major battle won by Jackson after the War of 1812 was officially over (1815)

Berlin Airlift: a Cold War mission; the U.S. flew supplies into West Berlin after the Soviets blocked the roads

Bill of Rights: the first ten amendments to the U.S. Constitution

Black Power: a 1960s African-American movement that promoted using force in the struggle for equal rights

Black Tuesday: October 29, 1929, the day the stock market crashed

Boston Massacre: a 1770 incident during which British soldiers killed several Americans

Boston Tea Party: a protest by colonists in 1773 against the British tax on tea; colonists dumped three shiploads of tea into Boston Harbor

Brown vs. Board of Education of Topeka: the Supreme Court ruling in 1954 that said schools must be integrated. This overturned the "separate but equal" ruling of *Plessy vs. Ferguson.*

cabinet: officials who head government agencies and advise the president

Cambodia: the country bordering Vietnam where American troops were sent in 1970

Camp David Accords: the peace agreement between Israel's Premier Begin and Egypt's President Sadat initiated by President Carter in 1979

Canal Zone: the strip of land leased by the U.S. from Panama where the Panama Canal is built

capitalism: an economic system; individuals control production of goods and government intervention is limited

carpetbagger: a Northerner who went to the South after the Civil War to profit financially

Central Powers: the World War I alliance between Germany and Austria-Hungary and later with Bulgaria and Turkey

checks and balances: the system in which the three branches of government have powers to limit the other branches so that no one branch becomes too powerful

Civil Rights Act of 1866: the law that made African Americans citizens of the United States

Civil Rights Act of 1875: the law that prohibited segregation of public places

Civil Rights Act of 1964: the law that made it easier and safer for African Americans to vote in the South and also prohibited racial discrimination in public facilities

Civil Rights Movement: the campaign in the 1960s to achieve equality for African Americans

Civil War (1861-1865): the conflict between the northern (Union) and southern (Confederate) states over the issues of slavery and states rights

Cold War: tensions between the U.S. and the Soviet Union after World War II

Confederate States of America: the association of 11 independent southern states formed after they seceded from the Union in 1860 and 1861

Congress: the legislative branch of government made up of the Senate and House of Representatives

Constitution: the written plan of government for the United States

containment policy: U.S. strategy aimed at limiting the spread of communism during the 1950s and 1960s

Cuban Missile Crisis: a 1962 confrontation between the U.S. and the Soviet Union over the building of Soviet missile bases in Cuba

D-Day: the beginning of the Allied invasion of France on June 6, 1944

Declaration of Independence: the document adopted by the Second Continental Congress in 1776 that declared American independence from Great Britain and listed the reasons for this action

deficit spending: paying out more public funds than are raised in taxes

deflation: a decline in prices caused by a decrease in money supply or spending

demilitarized zone: a zone or strip of land not controlled or used by the military

democracy: the form of government in which power is vested in the people and exercised by them through a system of free elections

department of state: the government bureau that advises the president on foreign relations

depression: a period of steep decline in business activity, usually marked by high levels of unemployment

disarmament: reduction or limitation in the number of weapons

domino theory: a key idea of U.S. foreign policy from the 1950s–1970s; belief that if a country fell to communism, the countries on its borders would also fall

economy: the system of producing, distributing, and consuming goods or services

Eighteenth Amendment: a constitutional change that prohibited the manufacture and sale of alcoholic beverages

elector: a person selected in a state to cast an electoral vote for president

Emancipation Proclamation: the decree issued by Abraham Lincoln in 1863 freeing the slaves in the Confederate states

Emergency Quota Act: a 1921 law that limited by nationality the number of immigrants to the United States

entrepreneur: a person who develops a business

Environmental Protection Agency (EPA): the department established in 1970 to monitor and reduce pollution

Equal Rights Amendment: a proposed constitutional amendment (1972) to provide equal rights for women

Espionage Act: 1917 law made it a crime to help enemy countries or to interfere with military recruitment

Fair Deal: President Truman's plan to extend New Deal programs

Fair Employment Practices Committee: a commission created in 1941 to prevent job discrimination against racial and ethnic groups and women

Fair Labor Standards Act: a 1938 law that outlawed child labor and set a forty-hour work week

favorable balance of trade: the situation in which a country exports more than it imports

Federal Highway Act: a 1956 law that provided federal funding for construction of interstate highways

Federal Reserve Act: a 1913 law that created a national banking system of twelve Federal Reserve Banks

Federal Reserve Board: the government agency that oversees the operation of the Federal Reserve System

Federal Securities Act: a 1933 law that regulates the way companies issue and sell stock

Federal Trade Commission: the agency created in 1914 to eliminate unfair business practices and enforce antitrust laws

Fifteenth Amendment: the constitutional amendment that guarantees all citizens the right to vote

First Amendment: the constitutional amendment that guarantees freedom of speech, religion, and the press, and the right to assemble peacefully

Fourteenth Amendment: the constitutional amendment that made African Americans citizens of their states as well as of the U.S., guaranteed their civil rights, and gave them equal protection of the laws

free enterprise: the economic system in which there is little government control over business practices

Gettysburg Address: the speech delivered by Abraham Lincoln in 1863

G.I. Bill of Rights: a program established in 1944 to provide low-cost loans to veterans

Gold Rush: the movement of 80,000 miners to California to look for gold in 1848

Great Awakening: a time of widespread religious fervor (in the 1740s)

Great Compromise: an agreement made at the Constitutional Convention in 1787 to create a House of Representatives elected by the people on the basis of population and a Senate elected by the state legislatures, two members from each state

Great Depression: the economic crisis from 1929 to 1940

Great Society: the social and economic programs of President Lyndon Johnson

Hiroshima: the Japanese city that was the site of the first atomic bombing by the U.S. in August, 1945

Ho Chi Minh Trail: a path running through Cambodia and Laos to South Vietnam that was used by the North Vietnamese as a supply trail during the Vietnam War

House of Representatives: the house of Congress in which states are represented according to their population

Housing Act: a law passed in 1961 that helped poor people pay their rent

human right: a privilege belonging to all human beings

immigrant: a person who comes to another country to live

Immigration Act of 1965: the law that changed admission quotas to the United States based on nationality

impeachment: formal charge of wrongdoing brought against an elected official of the federal government

imperialism: the practice of establishing and controlling colonies

Indian Rights Act (1968): a law passed to protect the rights of Native Americans

Industrial Revolution: the change in production methods in the early 1800s from human to machine power

inflation: the rise in prices

internationalism: a policy of cooperation among nations

Iron Curtain: the term Winston Churchill used to describe the division and tension between communist countries and the rest of the western world

isolationism: a national policy of maintaining a nation's interests without being involved with other countries

Jamestown: the first successful British colony in America

Jim Crow Law: any law that promoted segregation

Korean War: the war in 1950–52 between North and South Korea and their allies

Ku Klux Klan: a secret organization which terrorized African Americans

League of Nations: the international organization established in 1920 to seek world peace; dissolved in 1946 when the United Nations was formed

legislature: an elected body with the responsibility of making laws

Louisiana Purchase: land purchased from France by the United States in 1803 for $15 million; included all the land between the Mississippi River and the Rocky Mountains

Manhattan Project: the code name for the top-secret plan to develop the atom bomb

March on Washington (1963): a huge civil rights demonstration in Washington, D.C., during which Martin Luther King, Jr., delivered his "I Have a Dream" speech

Marshall Plan: the U.S. program for the economic recovery of Europe after World War II

Mason-Dixon line: the boundary between Maryland and Pennsylvania, traditional line between the North & South

McCarthyism: a period in the 1950s when many people were suspected of being Communists by Senator Joseph McCarthy

melting pot: the idea that immigrants of various cultural backgrounds gradually adapt to American ways

monopoly: exclusive control of a product or service which results in elimination of competition

Monroe Doctrine: a foreign policy statement that said the United States would not tolerate European interference in the Western Hemisphere

Montgomery Bus Boycott: a 1955 protest by blacks against Montgomery Alabama's segregation of city buses

Nagasaki: a Japanese city that was site of the second atomic bombing by the U.S. in 1945 which ended the war

National Aeronautics and Space Administration (NASA): the government agency responsible for space programs

National Association for the Advancement of Colored People (NAACP): the civil rights organization formed in 1909 to reduce discrimination against blacks and other people of color

nationalism: patriotic feelings for one's country

neutrality: the policy of avoiding ties with other nations or deep involvement in their affairs

New Deal: Franklin Roosevelt's program to revive the country from the Great Depression

New Frontier: John F. Kennedy's social and economic programs of the early 1960s

Nineteenth Amendment: the constitutional amendment in 1920 that gave women the right to vote

nominating convention: a meeting of party members to choose presidential and vice-presidential candidates

Normandy: the northern French province that was the site of the D-Day invasion during World War II

North Atlantic Treaty Organization (NATO): an agreement made in 1949 between the U.S., Great Britain, France, and eight other nations to protect against Soviet military threats

Open Door: an 1889 U.S. policy that assured all nations equal trade rights with China

oppressed: kept down by a harsh and unjust authority

Oregon Trail: the route followed by pioneers to the Northwest

Pacific Railway Act: a 1862 law authorizing construction of a railroad from Nebraska to the Pacific Coast

pacifist: a person who is against violence (and war)

patriot: a person who favored independence for the American colonies during the American Revolutionary period

peace movement: efforts made by organized groups to promote peace among nations

Peace of Paris: the 1783 agreement that ended the Revolutionary War

Pearl Harbor: a port in the Hawaiian Islands where the American Pacific fleet was destroyed by the Japanese in a surprise attack in 1941

Plymouth: the site in Massachusetts where the Pilgrims first landed in America in 1620

polio vaccine: an inoculation against polio developed by Dr. Jonas Salk

popular vote: a vote of the people

president: the elected head of the executive branch of government

primary elections: the process for selecting candidates to run for public office

propaganda: ideas spread in order to gain public support for a cause or to damage an opposing cause

public school: a school without tuition that is funded by taxes and open to all children

Puritans: English Protestants who came to America in the early 1600s for religious freedom

Quaker: a member of a pacifist religious sect which came to America seeking religious freedom

Reconstruction: the process of bringing the southern states back into the Union after the Civil War

Red Scare: the widespread fear of a communist takeover that swept the U.S. after World War II

referendum: a legal process by which the people can revoke a law passed by the legislature

Removal Law: a law passed in 1830 that provided money to help Native American tribes move west

reparations: money given by defeated nations as payment for damages suffered by other nations during a war

Rosa Parks: Alabama black woman arrested (1955) when she refused to give her seat on a bus to a white man

San Francisco Conference: the meeting held in 1945 to draft the United Nations Charter

secession: withdrawal from an association or group

segregation: separation of people on the basis of racial, religious, or social differences

Selective Service Act: the 1917 law that required the draft of men into military service for World War I

Senate: the house of Congress in which each state is represented by two senators

separatist: a person who withdrew or separated from the Church of England; also called a Pilgrim

Seventeenth Amendment: the constitutional amendment that provided for the election of senators by popular vote

Sixteenth Amendment: the constitutional amendment that gave Congress the power to levy an income tax

slave: a person who is owned by others (due to capture, purchase, or birth) and forced to work for them

Social Security Act: a 1935 law that created a system to provide old-age insurance and unemployment compensation

socialist: a person who believes in public ownership of all means of production and distribution of goods in an economy

states rights: the doctrine that holds that the states have powers that are not assigned to the federal government in the Constitution

Statue of Liberty: the statue in New York Harbor that was given to the United States by France

summit meeting: a meeting held between the heads of two countries to settle political issues

Supreme Court: the highest U.S. court of appeals, composed of nine justices

Taft-Hartley Labor Relations Act: the law passed in 1947 to regulate labor union activities and outlaw unfair practices by labor unions and employers

temperance: the movement to restrict the drinking of alcoholic beverages

Tennessee Valley Authority (TVA): a federal agency established in 1933 to develop the water-power resources of the Tennessee River Valley

Tet offensive: a major attack in 1968 on South Vietnamese cities by the North Vietnamese

third party: a political group organized to compete against the two major political parties

Thirteenth Amendment: the constitutional amendment that abolished slavery

Three Mile Island: the nuclear power plant near Harrisburg, Pennsylvania, that was the site of an accident in 1979

Truman Doctrine: the U.S. policy to give financial and military aid to nations so they could resist communist rule

trust: a group of corporations formed for the purpose of reducing competition

Twenty-First Amendment: the constitutional amendment that ended prohibition by repealing the Eighteenth Amendment

Twenty-Second Amendment: the constitutional amendment that said no one could hold the office of president for more than two terms

Twenty-Sixth Amendment: the constitutional amendment that gave 18- to 20-year-olds the right to vote

two-party system: a political system with two major parties of similar strength; in the U.S. these are now the Democratic and Republican parties

Underground Railroad: the system of people and processes for helping slaves escape to Canada

U-2 Affair: an incident in 1960 when an American spy plane was shot down during a mission over the USSR

V-E Day: May 8, 1945; the day when Germany surrendered to the Allies at the end of World War II

V-J Day: August 14, 1945; the day when Japan surrendered to the U.S., ending World War II

veto: the presidential power to reject bills passed by Congress

Viet Cong: South Vietnamese guerrilla soldiers who are pro-communist

Vietnam: the Southeast Asian country where the United States and South Vietnam forces fought a war against the communist North Vietnamese

Vietnamization: policy of building up the South Vietnamese army so that American troops could be withdrawn

Voting Rights Act: a law passed in 1965 that increased the number of African-American voters by putting an end to literacy tests and other practices used to keep African Americans from registering

war department: the bureau of government in charge of military affairs

Warren Court: the Supreme Court that passed important civil rights legislation under the liberal leadership of Chief Justice Warren from 1953 to 1968

Warsaw Pact: an alliance of Eastern European communist nations formed in response to NATO

Watergate Affair: a 1972 government scandal that led to the resignation of President Nixon in 1974

Women's Liberation Movement: the campaign of political action and demonstrations begun in the late 1960s aimed at attaining equal rights for women

Works Progress Administration (WPA): a New Deal agency that found useful work for unemployed persons

Wounded Knee: the site in South Dakota where Sioux Indian families were massacred by United States troops in 1891; also the site of a 1973 Native American protest

xenophobia: the fear of foreigners or strangers

Yalta Conference: a meeting in 1945 at Yalta between Churchill, Stalin, and Roosevelt to plan the defeat and occupation of Germany and German-occupied territories

UNITED STATES PRESIDENTS

	PRESIDENT	DATES IN OFFICE	PARTY	VICE PRESIDENT
1.	George Washington	1789-1797	None	John Adams
2.	John Adams	1797-1801	Federalist	Thomas Jefferson
3.	Thomas Jefferson	1801-1809	Republican	Aaron Burr
				George Clinton
4.	James Madison	1809-1817	Republican	George Clinton
				Elbridge Gerry
5.	James Monroe	1817-1825	Republican	Daniel D. Tompkins
6.	John Quincy Adams	1825-1829	Republican	John C. Calhoun
7.	Andrew Jackson	1829-1837	Democratic	John C. Calhoun
				Martin Van Buren
8.	Martin Van Buren	1837-1841	Democratic	Richard M. Johnson
9.	William Henry Harrison	1841	Whig	John Tyler
10.	John Tyler	1841-1845	Whig	
11.	James K. Polk	1845-1849	Democratic	George M. Dallas
12.	Zachary Taylor	1849-1850	Whig	Millard Fillmore
13.	Millard Fillmore	1850-1853	Whig	
14.	Franklin Pierce	1853-1857	Democratic	William R. King
15.	James Buchanan	1857-1861	Democratic	John C. Breckenridge
16.	Abraham Lincoln	1861-1865	Republican	Hannibal Hamlin
				Andrew Johnson
17.	Andrew Johnson	1865-1869	Republican	
18.	Ulysses S. Grant	1869-1877	Republican	Schuyler Colfax
				Henry Wilson
19.	Rutherford B. Hayes	1877-1881	Republican	William A. Wheeler
20.	James A. Garfield	1881	Republican	Chester A. Arthur
21.	Chester A. Arthur	1881-1885	Republican	
22.	Grover Cleveland	1885-1889	Democratic	Thomas P. Hendricks
23.	Benjamin Harrison	1889-1893	Republican	Levi P. Morton
24.	Grover Cleveland	1893-1897	Democratic	Adlai E. Stevenson
25.	William McKinley	1897-1901	Republican	Garrett A. Hobart
				Theodore Roosevelt
26.	Theodore Roosevelt	1901-1909	Republican	Charles W. Fairbanks
27.	William Howard Taft	1909-1913	Republican	James S. Sherman
28.	Woodrow Wilson	1913-1921	Democratic	Thomas R. Marshall
29.	Warren G. Harding	1921-1923	Republican	Calvin Coolidge
30.	Calvin Coolidge	1923-1929	Republican	Charles G. Dawes
31.	Herbert Hoover	1929-1933	Republican	Charles Curtis
32.	Franklin D. Roosevelt	1933-1945	Democratic	John Nance Garner
				Henry Wallace
				Harry S. Truman
33.	Harry S. Truman	1945-1953	Democratic	Alben W. Barkley
34.	Dwight D. Eisenhower	1953-1961	Republican	Richard M. Nixon
35.	John F. Kennedy	1961-1963	Democratic	Lyndon B. Johnson
36.	Lyndon B. Johnson	1963-1969	Democratic	Hubert H. Humphrey
37.	Richard M. Nixon	1969-1974	Republican	Spiro T. Agnew
				Gerald R. Ford
38.	Gerald R. Ford	1974-1977	Republican	Nelson Rockefeller
39.	Jimmy Carter	1977-1981	Democratic	Walter F. Mondale
40.	Ronald Reagan	1981-1989	Republican	George H. Bush
41.	George Bush	1989-1993	Republican	J. Danforth Quayle
42.	William J. Clinton	1993-2000	Democratic	Albert Gore

Basic Skills/U.S. History 6-8+

U.S. HISTORY TIMELINE

1492	Columbus Lands at San Salvador
1565	Spain Founds St. Augustine, Florida
1607	Founding of Jamestown
1620	Pilgrims Land at Plymouth
1754	French & Indian War Begins
1765	Stamp Act
1770	Boston Massacre
1772	Boston Tea Party
1774	First Continental Congress
1775	Battles of Concord & Lexington
1775	Second Continental Congress
1776	Declaration of Independence
1783	Treaty of Paris
1788	Ratification of Constitution
1789	George Washington Inaugurated
1812	War of 1812 against Britain
1823	Monroe Doctrine
1845	Texas Annexed
1846	Mexican War
1849	California Gold Rush
1853	Gadsden Purchase
1857	*Dred Scott* Decision
1860	South Carolina Secedes from Union
1861	Confederacy Forms; Civil War Begins
1864	Civil War Ends
1865	Lincoln Assassinated
1867	Reconstruction Act
1868	Andrew Johnson Impeached
1870	Industrial Revolution
1877	End of Reconstruction
1881	President Garfield Assassinated
1890	Sherman Antitrust Act
1891	Populist Party Begins
1896	*Plessy vs Ferguson* Decision
1898	Spanish-American War Begins
1900	Open Door Policy for China
1900	Waves of Immigrants Arrive in U.S.
1901	McKinley Assassinated
1913	Federal Reserve Act
1914	Panama Canal Opened
1914	World War I Begins
1917	U.S. Enters World War I
1918	End of World War I
1919	Prohibition Begins
1920	19th Amendment (Women's Vote)
1924	Teapot Dome Scandal
1929	Stock Market Crash
1929	Great Depression Begins
1933	Hitler Comes to Power in Germany
1935	Social Security Act
1939	World War II Begins
1941	Japanese Bomb Pearl Harbor
1941	U.S. Enters World War II
1944	D-Day
1945	Roosevelt Dies
1945	Yalta Conference
1945	U.S. Drops Atomic Bombs on Japan
1945	World War II Ends
1945	UN Charter Approved
1947	Marshall Plan
1947	Cold War Begins
1948	Berlin Airlift
1949	Formation of NATO
1950	Korean War Begins
1954	*Brown vs Board of Education* Decision
1956	Suez Canal Crisis
1957	Sputnik Launched
1959	Castro Becomes Dictator in Cuba
1961	Berlin Wall Built
1962	Cuban Missile Crisis
1963	Kennedy Assassinated
1964	Civil Rights Act
1965	U.S. Involvement in Vietnam Increases
1968	M.L. King, Jr., Assassinated
1968	Robert Kennedy Assassinated
1969	U.S. Lands on Moon
1970	U.S. Troops Invade Cambodia
1972	Watergate
1973	*Roe vs Wade* Decision
1974	Nixon Resigns
1975	South Vietnam Falls to North Vietnam
1979	Camp David Accord Signed
1979	Three Mile Island Nuclear Disaster
1979	U.S. Hostages Seized in Iran
1981	Sandra Day O'Connor Appointed to Supreme Court
1985	Gorbachev Becomes USSR Premier
1986	Iran-Contra Affair
1989	U.S. Invades Panama
1989	Berlin Wall Falls
1989	Democratic Movements In Eastern Europe
1990	Launch of Hubbell Space Telescope
1991	Breakup of Soviet Union
1991	Gulf War
1992	Los Angeles Riots Sparked by Rodney King Verdict
1993	Israeli-Palestinian Peace Agreement
1995	Oklahoma City Courthouse Bombing
1996	Bombing in Atlanta at Olympics

Copyright ©1997 by Incentive Publications, Inc., Nashville, TN.

U.S. HISTORY SKILLS TEST

Each correct answer is worth 1 point.

For 1–8, give the letter on the map that gives the location of the answer to each question.

_____ 1. Which was the first colony formed?

_____ 2. Which colony was known as New Sweden?

_____ 3. Which colony was founded by the Puritan preacher, Roger Williams?

_____ 4. Which colony's major crop was tobacco?

_____ 5. Which was a Quaker colony founded by William Penn?

_____ 6. Which colony was founded as a home for people who couldn't pay their debts?

_____ 7. Which colony was known as New Netherland?

_____ 8. Which was the colony of South Carolina?

For 9–23, write the letter of the item associated with the person.

____ 9. LaSalle
____ 10. J. P. Morgan
____ 11. Jonas Salk
____ 12. Rosa Parks
____ 13. Geraldine Ferraro
____ 14. Richard Nixon
____ 15. Harriet Beecher Stowe
____ 16. Franklin D. Roosevelt
____ 17. Lyndon Johnson
____ 18. Sandra Day O'Connor
____ 19. John F. Kennedy
____ 20. William Penn
____ 21. General MacArthur
____ 22. Joseph McCarthy
____ 23. Clara Barton

A. Louisiana Purchase
B. segregated bus
C. New Deal
D. vice-presidential candidate
E. polio
F. Pennsylvania
G. bombing of North Vietnam
H. Supreme Court
I. *Uncle Tom's Cabin*
J. Korean War
K. Cuban Missile Crisis
L. American Red Cross
M. communist scare
N. U.S. Steel Company
O. Watergate

For 24–33, write the letter that shows the place where each event took place. Then write the name of the state.

_____ 24. Salem Witch Trials
_____

_____ 25. Battle of New Orleans
_____

_____ 26. End of Civil War
_____

_____ 27. Gold Rush
_____

_____ 28. last spike of transcontinental railroad
_____

_____ 29. Bay of Pigs Invasion
_____

_____ 30. 1957 attempt to integrate a Little Rock High School
_____

_____ 31. Purchase from Russia in 1867
_____

_____ 32. Object of "54–40 or Fight!" Campaign
_____

_____ 33. Battle of Little Bighorn
_____

Name _____

Basic Skills/U.S. History 6-8+

For 34–43, write the letter of the correct answer on the line.

_____ 34. Christopher Columbus's 1492 voyage was sponsored by the Queen and King of
a. Great Britain
b. Spain
c. Italy
d. Portugal

_____ 35. Puritans and Pilgrims came to the New World in search of
a. escape from prison
b. political freedom
c. profit
d. gold
e. religious freedom

_____ 36. Which is NOT associated with the American Revolution?
a. Battle of Little Bighorn
b. Battle of Bunker Hill
c. Boston Tea Party
d. Stamp Act

_____ 37. Which of these was a reason for the War of 1812?
a. Britain forced taxes on the United States.
b. Canada was trying to take land away from the United States.
c. U.S. sailors were being kidnapped and forced to serve in the British Navy
d. United States wanted to gain land from Mexico

_____ 38. Which amendment to the Constitution abolished slavery?
a. 1st   b. 20th   c. 19th   d. 13th

_____ 39. Which was a provision of the Reconstruction Act after the Civil War?
a. States could join the Union when 10% of the voters swore loyalty to the Union.
b. Union soldiers were stationed in southern states to protect the rights of freed slaves.
c. All persons were free from slavery.
d. Blacks were kept in a state of semi-slavery.

_____ 40. Which territory was NOT gained by the U.S. at the end of the Spanish-American War?
a. Florida
b. Cuba
c. Puerto Rico
d. Guam
e. Philippines

_____ 41. Which country was NOT a part of the Allied Forces in World War II?
a. Italy
b. France
c. United States
d. Soviet Union
e. Great Britain

_____ 42. Which was NOT a part of the New Deal?
a. Social Security Act
b. Medicare
c. Works Progress Administration
d. Brain Trust

_____ 43. The alliance among the U.S. and European Nations that developed after World War II to protect against Soviet aggression was:
a. The Warsaw Pact
b. United Nations
c. NATO
d. Allied Forces
e. Axis Powers

For 44–48, write the letter from one of the two maps that shows each location.

_____ 44. The part of Korea that has a communist government

Name _____

_____ 45. The country of China

_____ 46. The area of Vietnam ruled by Ho Chi Minh during the Vietnam War

_____ 47. The country of Cambodia

_____ 48. The country supported by the U.S. in the Vietnam War

For 49–63, match each term with its description from the list below. Write the correct letter.

_____ 49. indigenous

_____ 50. CIO

_____ 51. Mayflower Compact

_____ 52. Louisiana Purchase

_____ 53. Articles of Confederation

_____ 54. The *Merrimac*

_____ 55. Cheyenne

_____ 56. Bill of Rights

_____ 57. Stamp Acts

_____ 58. Monroe Doctrine

_____ 59. underground railroad

_____ 60. *Plessy vs Ferguson*

_____ 61. *Brown vs the Board of Education*

_____ 62. Jim Crow Laws

_____ 63. U-2 Affair

A. 1803 sale of western land to U.S. by France

B. Government document of 13 colonies

C. Great Plains Indian tribe

D. system for helping slaves escape to Canada

E. court decision for integration

F. native to an area

G. Union warship captured in the Civil War

H. policy that U.S. would not tolerate European interference in the western hemisphere

I. American spy plane shot down over Soviet Union

J. large labor union

K. British law taxing printed material in colonies

L. Pilgrim document for self-government

M. first 10 amendments of the Constitution

N. laws promoting segregation

O. "separate but equal" court decision

For 64–73, write the letter from the map that shows the location of each landmark or important place in U.S. history below. Then write the name of the state where that landmark is found.

_____ 64. Liberty Bell _____

_____ 65. Pearl Harbor _____

_____ 66. Fort Sumter _____

_____ 67. Alamo _____

_____ 68. Grand Canyon_____

_____ 69. Wounded Knee _____

_____ 70. Great Salt Lake _____

_____ 71. Gateway Arch _____

_____ 72. Pike's Peak _____

_____ 73. Niagara Falls _____

For 74–85, write the letter that shows where each event would be placed on the timeline below.

_____ 74. Founding of Georgia

_____ 75. World War I Begins

_____ 76. Great Depression

_____ 77. French & Indian War

_____ 78. World War II Begins

_____ 79. Korean War

_____ 80. Indian Removal Act

_____ 81. Declaration of Independence

_____ 82. Vietnam War Ends

_____ 83. Transcontinental Railroad

_____ 84. Founding of United Nations

_____ 85. Civil War Ends

For 86–95, write the letter of the correct answer on the line.

_____ 86. Which was a cause of the Korean War?
   a. North Korea invaded South Korea.
   b. South Korea invaded North Korea.
   c. Japan attacked North Korea.
   d. The United States invaded North Korea.

_____ 87. Which statement is NOT true of the Vietnam War?
   a. Thousands of Americans protested the war.
   b. U.S. troops also bombed and invaded Cambodia.
   c. U.S. and South Vietnam won the war.
   d. In the Tet Offensive, North Vietnam attacked many South Vietnamese cities.

_____ 88. Which United States space program landed a man on the moon?
   a. Gemini
   b. Mercury
   c. Challenger
   d. Apollo

_____ 89. Which woman was the first vice-presidential candidate?
   a. Coretta Scott King
   b. Geraldine Ferraro
   c. Sandra Day O'Connor
   d. Ruth Bader Ginsberg

_____ 90. Which was NOT an event of the 1960's?
   a. Assassination of John F. Kennedy
   b. Assassination of Martin Luther King
   c. Woodstock
   d. Killing of students at Kent State University

_____ 91. Which came last?
   a. Korean War
   b. Persian Gulf War
   c. World War II
   d. Vietnam War

_____ 92. Who was president immediately following Dwight Eisenhower?
   a. Kennedy
   b. Truman
   c. Nixon
   d. Johnson

_____ 93. Which came first?
   a. U.S. moonwalk
   b. Martin Luther King assassination
   c. End of Cold War
   d. Great Depression

_____ 94. Which came first?
   a. Watergate Affair
   b. End of Vietnam War
   c. Kennedy assassination
   d. Fall of Berlin Wall

_____ 95. Which of these presidencies came 3rd of the 4?
   a. Abraham Lincoln
   b. Dwight Eisenhower
   c. Franklin Roosevelt
   d. Teddy Roosevelt

For 96–100, match each letter with the organization it describes.
   A. works against discrimination for minorities
   B. U.S. space research and exploration
   C. alliance of U.S. and European nations
   D. problem-solving and peace-keeping group of many nations
   E. powerful labor union

_____ 96. NATO

_____ 97. UN

_____ 98. NASA

_____ 99. AFL-CIO

_____ 100. NAACP

SCORE: Total Points _____ out of a possible 100 points

Name _____

U.S. HISTORY
SKILLS TEST ANSWER KEY

1. E	34. b	68. A—Arizona
2. B	35. e	69. C—South Dakota
3. H	36. a	70. G—Utah
4. F	37. c	71. D—Missouri
5. A	38. d	72. E—Colorado
6. C	39. b	73. F—New York
7. G	40. a	74. Q
8. D	41. a	75. R
9. A	42. b	76. Z
10. N	43. c	77. P
11. E	44. E	78. Y
12. B	45. B	79. X
13. D	46. A	80. O
14. O	47. C	81. S
15. I	48. D	82. W
16. C	49. F	83. T
17. G	50. J	84. V
18. H	51. L	85. U
19. K	52. A	86. a
20. F	53. B	87. c
21. J	54. G	88. d
22. M	55. C	89. b
23. L	56. M	90. d
24. E—Massachusetts	57. K	91. b
25. F—Louisiana	58. H	92. a
26. G—Virginia	59. D	93. d
27. A—California	60. O	94. c
28. H—Utah	61. E	95. c
29. B—Cuba	62. N	96. D
30. I—Arkansas	63. I	97. C
31. C—Alaska	64. I—Pennsylvania	98. B
32. J—Oregon	65. B—Hawaii	99. E
33. D—Montana	66. J—South Carolina	100. A
	67. H—Texas	

ANSWERS

page 10

1. 30,000
2. Asia
3. Alaska
4. Bering Strait
5. Ice Ages
6. glaciers
7. land bridge
8-9. people, animals
10. 1000
11. Viking
12. Atlantic
13. Norway
14. Canada
15. Newfoundland
16. Leif Ericson
17. 500
18. Christopher Columbus
19. Italy
20. China
21. Indies
22. Atlantic
23. Isabella
24. Ferdinand
25. Spain
26. 1492
27. San Salvador
28. Cuba
29. Hispaniola
30-31. Haiti, Dominican Republic

page 11

Answers will vary.

Page 12

Across
5. Drake
6. Amerigo
7. La Salle
11. Treaty of Tordesillas
13. France
15. Columbus
16. Coronado

Down
1. John Cabot
2. Verrazano
3. Champlain
4. California
8. St. Lawrence
9. Mississippi
10. Henry Hudson
12. Elizabeth
14. Florida

Page 13

1. What was religious freedom?
2. What was Jamestown?
3. What were (any 4 of these) . . . Boston, New York, Baltimore, Charleston, Savannah, Philadelphia?
4. Who was Captain John Smith of Jamestown?
5. Who was Virginia Dare?
6. Who were the slaves and indentured servants?
7. What were the Appalachian Mountains?
8. What was the Mayflower Compact?
9. What was Maryland?
10. What was New Amsterdam?
11. What was Sweden?
12. Who were William Penn, James Oglethorpe, Sir George Calvert, Lord John Berkeley, Thomas Hooker, and Roger Williams?

Page 14

I–IV. Check student maps for accuracy.
1. Massachusetts
2. Virginia
3. Delaware
4. Rhode Island
5. Massachusetts
6. Virginia, Maryland
7. New York
8. Georgia
9. Virginia
10. Pennsylvania
11. North Carolina, South Carolina
12. Georgia
13. Massachusetts

Page 15

I. Religious Freedom:
Massachusetts
Connecticut
Rhode Island
New Jersey
Pennsylvania
Maryland
North Carolina
South Carolina
Profit & Trade:
New Hampshire
Connecticut
New York
Delaware
New Jersey
Pennsylvania
Virginia
Maryland
North Carolina
South Carolina
Georgia
Political Freedom:
Connecticut
New Jersey
Pennsylvania
Maryland
Home for Debtors:
Georgia
II. Answers will vary.

Page 16

Answers will vary. Students should find general information about the Salem Witch Trials which took place in Salem Village, Massachusetts in 1692. The Puritans believed that witchcraft was the work of the devil. Two young girls in the household of Rev. Parris complained of sharp pains and attributed them to spells cast upon them by women in the community. Stories of witchcraft had been told to the young girls by Tituba, a West Indian slave. The hysteria that followed led to about 500 people being accused of witchcraft. Many of the accused were tortured. 27 were convicted, 19 were hanged, and several more were imprisoned.

Page 17

1. George Washington
2. Duquesne
3. Necessity
4. militia
5. General Braddock
6. Iroquois
7. Britain
8. Montcalm
9. Oswego
10. Ontario
11. William Henry
12. William Pitt
13. Amherst
14. Louisbourg
15. Forks of the Ohio
16. Ticonderoga
17. Quebec
18. Paris Treaty
19. east
20. Revolution

Page 18

3	Boston Tea Party, 12/16/1773
11	First U.S. Submarine (*Turtle*), 9/6/1776
19	Constitutional Convention, 5/25/1787
12	Battle of Trenton, 12/19/1776
7	Ride of Dawes, Prescott, & Revere, 4/18/1775
5	The Quartering Act, 6/2/1774
14	Battle of Saratoga, 9/19/1777
10	Declaration of Independence, 7/4/1776
1	The Stamp Act, 11/1/1765
2	The Boston Massacre, 3/5/1770
8	Battle of Lexington and Concord, 4/19/1775
20	Washington's Farewell Address, 9/17/1796
16	Articles of Confederation, 3/1/1781
9	Battle of Bunker Hill (Breed's Hill), 6/17/1775
6	First Continental Congress, 9/1774 to 10/1774

13 Washington crosses the Delaware, 12/22/1776
17 Cornwallis surrenders at Yorktown, 10/19/1781
4   Intolerable Acts, 3/31/1774
18 The Treaty of Paris, 9/13/1783
15 Winter at Valley Forge, 12/19/1777 to 6/19/1778

Page 19

Answers will vary.

Page 20

Answers may vary somewhat.

Who?   U.S. President Thomas Jefferson and France's Napoleon
       Also: Livingston, Monroe, Tallyrand

What? Louisiana territory purchased from France, original idea was to purchase New Orleans and North Florida for $2 million

When? 1803 after France lost control of Haiti following a slave revolt

Where? New Orleans, up the Mississippi River to the Rocky Mountains and north to Canada

Why?   Jefferson wanted to be sure that the American farmers would have the ability to ship goods through the port of New Orleans

How?   U.S. purchased from France for $15 million because Napoleon needed the money to finance wars in Europe.

1. Spain
2. doubled
3. Yes; expanded the president's role to include the ability to purchase territory; the purchase doubled the size of the U.S.
4. He needed money to pay for wars in Europe.
5. New Orleans; it gave a water connection from the Gulf of Mexico to the Great Plains.

Page 21

1. James Madison
2. Great Britain, France
3. War Hawks
4. neutrality
5. American ships
6. British navy
7. Great Britain
8. Canada
9. Great Britain
10. Canada
11. *Constitution*
12. Chesapeake
13. Washington
14. "Old Ironsides"
15. "Star Spangled Banner"

16. Dolly Madison
17. Battle of New Orleans
18. Andrew Jackson

Page 22

Answers may vary somewhat.

1. The Appalachian Mountains; the discovery of the Cumberland Pass (and/or the invention of the Conestoga Wagon)
2. The Louisiana Purchase; allowed settlers to travel by river to new lands, increased the amount of land available for settlement
3. Area of upper midwest ceded by Great Britain—1818
   Florida ceded by Spain—1819
   Gadsden Purchase—1853
4. Americans in Texas rebelled against Mexican rule; Texas was independent for about 10 years; In 1844 President Sam Houston of Texas signed Treaty of Annexation; 1845 U.S. Congress passed a resolution admitting Texas into the Union.
5. Answers will vary.
6. Oregon; Britain; Line at 49° latitude gave land south of the line to U.S. and lands north of the line to Britain
7. This was a result of the Indian Removal Act. Cherokees were forced to march 116 days to Oklahoma. 1 out of every 4 of the Cherokees died on the trip.
8. All or parts of: California, Nevada, Utah, Arizona, New Mexico, Colorado, Wyoming
9. Opening of Santa Fe Trail—1821
   Erie Canal completed—1825
   Purchase of Alaska—1867
   Transcontinental Railroad—1869

Page 23

Across	Down
3. indigo	1. newspaper
4. *Uncle Tom's Cabin*	2. Sojourner
	3. industry
8. secede	4. underground
9. freedom	5. Compromiser
11. guns	6. slave codes
12. illegal	7. abolitionists
17. Tubman	10. Mott
18. slave	13. liberty
20. Dred Scott	14. chattel
22. cotton	15. farmers
23. rice	16. fifteen
24. Whitney	19. Turner
	21. Stowe

Page 24

Answers will vary somewhat.

1. The *Dred Scott* case
2. Formation of the Confederacy (6 states secede from Union)
3. Abraham Lincoln inaugurated

4. Civil War begins
5. Battle of Bull Run
6. Many people in North and West sympathize with the South and oppose the war (they are called "copperheads")
7. The Emancipation Proclamation
8. Battle of Gettysburg
9. Lincoln's Gettysburg Address
10. Burning of Atlanta by Union forces
11. Destruction of Confederate capital of Richmond
12. End of Civil War (Lee surrenders to Grant at Appomattox Courthouse)

Page 25

Answers will vary somewhat.

Lincoln: President after the war; assassinated in 1865

Black Codes: laws passed by southern states to control newly freed blacks

10% Plan: Lincoln's plan for reconstruction (When 10% of each state's voters swore loyalty to the Union, they could form a state government.)

Freedman's Bureau: organization set up by Congress to help the freed slaves

carpetbagger: Northerners who moved to the South after the war to profit financially; the term was considered an epithet as many Southern conservatives thought they were political and financial opportunists

Revels & Bruce: first blacks elected to the U.S. Senate

1866 Civil Rights Act: law that made blacks citizens of the U.S.

1867 Reconstruction Act: said the South would be ruled by the Union Army until state governments were formed run by blacks and whites who had been loyal to the Union

Andrew Johnson: U.S. president from 1865–1869, the only U.S. president to be impeached (but not convicted)

Booth: man who assassinated President Lincoln

Ku Klux Klan: secret white supremacist group formed to hold blacks down by terror

sharecropping: tenant farmers who received credit for seed, tools, living quarters, etc. from their landowners; after their crops were harvested they received an agreed percentage of the profit minus their credit charges

impeachment: bringing charges against a president to remove him

13th Amendment: officially abolished slavery

14th Amendment: defined citizen as any person born or naturalized in the U.S.

15th Amendment: gave all citizens (including blacks) the right to vote

Page 26
1. Oregon
2. Alaska
3. Rio Grande
4. Gadsden
5. Land
6. Mexican War
7. gold
8. Mississippi; Rocky
9. homesteaders
10. transcontinental railroad
11. Any four of these: Sioux, Comanche, Crow, Blackfoot, Cheyenne, Pawnee, Arapaho, Wichita, Kiowa, Kansa Osage, Hidatsa
12. reservations
13. Cuba; Puerto Rico; Guam; Philippines
14. Hawaii

Page 27
1. H. Alger
2. W. McAllister
3. J. P. Morgan
4. J. D. Rockefeller
5. W. S. Burroughs
6. A. Carnegie
7. H. Bessemer, W. Kelly
8. T. A. Edison
9. A. G. Bell
10. C. Sholes
11. J. F. Duryea
12. E. L. Drake
13. C. Vanderbilt
14. L. Stanford
15. G. T. Woods

Page 28

A.	1	E.	4	I.	12	M.	14
B.	5	F.	2	J.	13	N.	8
C.	7	G.	6	K.	10	O.	3
D.	15	H.	11	L.	9		

Page 29
See that student has found all of these words in the puzzle.
1. homesteaders
2. transcontinental
3. Central Pacific; Union Pacific
4. Charles Crocker
5. reservation
6. spike
7. golden
8. Little Bighorn
9. Sitting Bull; Crazy Horse
10. Pike's Peak
11. Promontory Point
12. Dodge
13. ranches
14. gold
15. brand
16. buffalo; bison
17. Chisholm

18. Joseph
19. Chinese
20. lasso; saddle

Pages 30–31
1. Allied Powers
   Leading Powers:
   Great Britain
   France
   Russia
   Others:

Albania	Montenegro
Belgium	Portugal
Greece	Romania
Ireland	Serbia
Italy	United States
Japan	most of
Luxembourg	North Africa

2. Central (Axis) Powers
   Austria-Hungary
   Germany
   Ottoman Empire (Turkey)
   Bulgaria
3. Neutral countries

Norway	Spain
Sweden	Netherlands
Switzerland	
Denmark	

5. Answers will vary. Some possibilities:
   Causes:
   1. Leaders of industrial countries wanted to increase their power and landholdings
   2. Nationalism—people with common languages wanted to throw off foreign rule.
   3. Imperialism—European nations wanted colonies in Africa, Asia, and the Pacific.
   4. Militarism—European nations expanded their navies and armies and had the ability to take over other lands.
   5. Rival Alliances—Triple Entente and Triple Alliance opposed and mistrusted each other.
   6. Assassination of Austro-Hungarian Prince, Archduke Ferdinand by a Serb nationalist
   Effects:
   1. U.S. Congress passed Selective Service Act
   2. Germany became a republic
   3. U.S. president proposed a peace plan and the League of Nations
   4. Germany was humiliated
   5. New nations were created in Eastern Europe

See that student has correctly shaded and labeled items on the map.

Page 32
Answers will vary.

Page 33
1. gold
2. crash
3. prosperity
4. migrant
5. Black Tuesday
6. FDR
7. New Deal
8. unemployment
9. Hoovervilles
10. federal
11. Bonus March
12. Dust Bowl
13. soup kitchens
14. Hoover
15. Panic

Page 34
True of New Deal:
1, 2, 5, 7, 8, 10, 11, 12, 14, 15, 19, 20

Page 35

3/15/39	Hitler occupies Czechoslovakia.
9/3/39	Britain and France declare war on Germany; U.S. remains neutral.
3/29/40	Soviet Union announces its neutrality.
6/22/40	France surrenders to Germany.
7/10/40	Battle of Britain begins.
5/27/41	The British Navy sinks the German warship, Bismarck.
12/7/41	Japan bombs Pearl Harbor, Hawaii.
12/8/41	U.S. declares war on Japan.
12/11/41	Germany and Italy declare war on the U.S.
6/6/42	Allies win battle of Midway in the South Pacific.
6/19/42	Roosevelt and Churchill meet in U.S.
11/8/42	Allied troops land in Algeria and Morocco.
7/10/43	Invasion of Italy begins.
10/1/43	Allies capture Naples, Italy.
11/22/43	Allies capture Tarawa Island in the Pacific.
3/24/44	U.S. victory in Solomon Islands.
8/25/44	Paris, France is liberated by Allies.
1/28/45	Battle of the Bulge ends.
3/16/45	U.S. Marines capture Iwo Jima.
4/12/45	President Roosevelt dies; Truman becomes president of the U.S.
4/20/45	U.S. captures Nuremberg, Germany.
5/7/45	Germany surrenders.
6/22/45	U.S. captures Okinawa in Pacific.
8/6/45	U.S. drops atomic bomb on Hiroshima, Japan.
8/9/45	U.S. drops atomic bomb on Nagasaki, Japan.
9/2/45	Japan signs surrender.

Page 36

1. C, E	5. C, E	9. E, C
2. E, C	6. C, E	10. C, E
3. C, E	7. E, C	11. E, C
4. E, C	8. E, C	

Page 37

Answers will vary.

Page 38

Check to see that student has labeled map correctly.

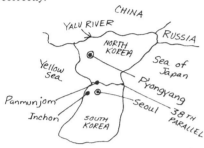

Page 39

Across	Down
3. debate	1. Kennedy
4. Corps	2. hippies
5. Great	6. Missile
9. Bay of Pigs	Crisis
10. Wounded	7. commune
11. Woodstock	8. Kent
14. NOW	9. boycott
15. Medicare	12. Vietnam
16. Clay	13. King
17. Rights	16. Cubans
18. Armstrong	
19. assassins	

Page 40

1. military	7. Nixon
2. killed	8. protesters
3. Kennedy	9. Cambodia
4. Johnson	10. Kent State
5. troops	11. Peace
6. Saigon	12. Khmer Rouge

Page 41

1. astronauts
2. moon
3. scrub
4. *Challenger*
5. Armstrong
6. Cosmonaut
7. *Sputnik*
8. Orbit
9. satellite
10. probe
11. docking
12. Liftoff
13. reentry
14. pad
15. Glenn

16. Apollo
17. NASA

Page 42

Please see page 54.

Page 43

1. Sacagawea
2. Harriet Tubman
3. Coretta Scott King
4. Eleanor Roosevelt
5. Helen Keller
6. Wilma Mankiller
7. Liliuokalani
8. Sally Ride
9. Sandra Day O'Connor
10. Amelia Earhart
11. Rosalyn Sussman Yalow
12. Louisa May Alcott
13. Geraldine Ferraro
14. Rosa Parks
15. Clara Barton
16. Harriet Beecher Stowe
17. Ruth Ginsberg
18. Florence Griffith Joyner

Page 44

1. Johnson
2. unconstitutional
3. citizenship
4. guaranteed
5. deprive
6. liberty
7. discrimination
8. Robinson
9. segregating
10. integration
11. Eisenhower
12. Rosa Parks
13. Montgomery
14. clergyman
15. voice

Page 45

1. E	7. N	13. G
2. K	8. S	14. M
3. H	9. Q	15. R
4. O	10. C	16. B
5. A	11. L	17. P
6. I	12. D	18. J

Pages 46–47

1. New Jersey
2. Oregon
3. Tennessee
4. Pennsylvania
5. Louisiana
6. Alabama
7. Hawaii
8. Minnesota
9. Kentucky
10. South Carolina
11. Wyoming

12. Ohio
13. Massachusetts
14. Florida
15. Colorado
16. Iowa
17. New Mexico
18. Arkansas
19. Maine
20. Virginia
21. Delaware
22. Nevada
23. North Dakota
24. Illinois
25. Alaska
26. Texas
27. Maryland
28. Oklahoma
29. Georgia
30. Arizona
31. Connecticut
32. California
33. Kansas
34. Wisconsin
35. Mississippi
36. Idaho
37. North Carolina
38. Indiana
39. Washington
40. Vermont
41. Michigan
42. Rhode Island
43. Montana
44. West Virginia
45. New York
46. Missouri
47. Utah
48. South Dakota
49. New Hampshire
50. Nebraska

Page 48

Across
4. telegraph
5. Microsoft
7. typewriter
8. Kodak camera
10. phonograph
12. automobile
13. plastic
14. shoemaking
16. sleeping car
18. cotton gin

Down
1. razor
2. polio
3. telephone
6. sewing machine
9. air flight
11. plow
14. stove
15. reaper
17. pen